ALASKA

ALASKA BY ROAD

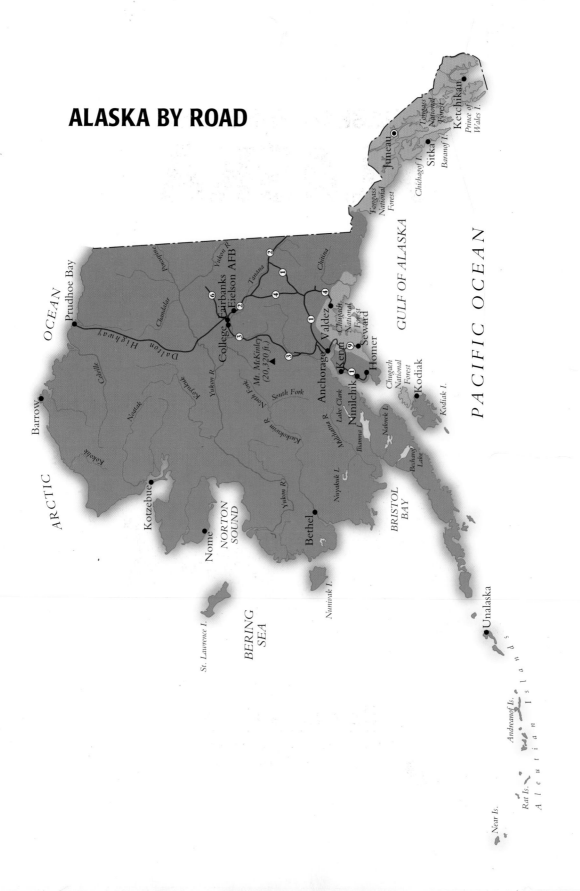

CELEBRATE THE STATES
ALASKA

Rebecca Stefoff

BENCHMARK BOOKS

MARSHALL CAVENDISH
NEW YORK

Benchmark Books
Marshall Cavendish Corporation
99 White Plains Road
Tarrytown, New York 10591-9001

Library of Congress Cataloging-in-Publication Data
Stefoff, Rebecca, date.
Alaska / Rebecca Stefoff.
p.   cm. — (Celebrate the states)
Includes bibliographical references and index.
Summary: A profile of the biggest state, including its geography, history, economy,
population, resources, famous citizens, and places of interest to visit.
ISBN 0-7614-0207-1
1. Alaska—Juvenile literature. [1. Alaska.] I. Title. II. Series.
F904.3.S76   1998   917.98—dc21   96-49313   CIP   AC

Maps and graphics supplied by Oxford Cartographers, Oxford, England

Photo research by Ellen Barrett Dudley and Matthew J. Dudley

Cover photo: *Ken Graham Agency*, Dicon Joseph

The photographs in this book are used by permission and through the courtesy of: *The Image Bank*: Michael Melford, 6-7; Joseph Van, 31; Cara Moore, 63; Harald Sund, 67 (top), 105, 106, 135, back cover; John Lewis Stage, 67 (bottom); Nick Nicholson, 76; Paul McCormick, 78, 116; Timothy A. Murphy, 100. *Ken Graham Agency*: David Job, 10-11, 108; Steven Nourse, 20, 27; Ken Graham, 23, 51, 54-55, 62, 64, 65, 128; Kim Heacox, 72-73; Doug Ogden, 109 (bottom); Leo Keeler, 118-119. *Photo Researchers, Inc.*: Michael Giannechini, 13, 109 (top), 111, 121 (bottom); Francois Gohier, 15; Ron Sanford, 19; Jack Finch/Science Photo Library, 24; Dan Guravich, 26, 61; Renee Lynn, 29, 83; Tibor Hirsch, 71; Lawrence Migdale, 79, 86; William Bacon, 82; Jim Cartier/Science Source, 85; Mark Newman, 88, 112; Gordon Gahan, 90-91; Frans Lanting, 102-103; Vanessa Vick, 113, 127; Charlie Ott, 121 (top); Tom & Pat Leeson, 124. *Anchorage Museum of History and Art*: 32-33 (# 80.115.1), 37 (# 82.84.1), 59 (# B78. 180.132); 94 (# 88.39.1). *Archives, Alaska and Polar Regions Dept., University of Alaska, Fairbanks*: Litka Atlas, Rare Books Collection (C0024), 35, 36, 41 (bottom); 41 (top) (# 68-12-56N); Lulu Fairbanks Photograph Collection, 48 (# 68-69-1194N); Historical Photograph Collection, 131 (# 67-44-3N). *University of Alaska Museum, Fairbanks*: 39. *Alaska State Museum, Juneau*: 42 (V-A-142). *Special Collections Division, University of Washington Libraries*: 43 (neg# Cantwell 46). *Reuters/Corbis-Bettmann*: 52, 98. *Corbis-Bettmann*: 93, 130, 133 (left). *Alaska State Library, Early Prints of Alaska*: 96 (PCA 01-4332), 133 (right) (PCA 01- 3294). *Reuters/02/Archive Photos*: 134.

Printed in Italy

3   5   6   4   2

CONTENTS

ALASKA IS....

Denali National Park

Alaska is the biggest state in the United States . . .

"Alaska should have been a nation. It's too majestic, too massive to be a mere state."

—Walter "Wally" Hickel, twice governor of Alaska

"The central paradox of Alaska is that it is as small as it is large— an immense landscape with so few people in it that language is stretched to call it a frontier, let alone a state."

—John McPhee, *Coming into the Country*

. . . and the farthest north.

"This place is *cold!* Just plain cold. I didn't think a place could get this cold. Yowee!"

—visitor from Pennsylvania experiencing winter in Fairbanks

Alaska is both glorious and harsh.

"To the lover of pure wilderness Alaska is one of the most wonderful countries in the world."

—naturalist John Muir, *Travels in Alaska* (1915)

"This country'll kill you if you're stupid. Or just unlucky."

—park ranger, Gates of the Arctic National Park and Preserve

Its people struggle to balance the old and the new . . .

"We've lost our culture. . . . Our old ways are going, going, gone."

—Roy Huhndorf, head of Cook Inlet Region Native Corporation

"I liked the life we used to live a long time ago, but we were always in need of something. I would say we live in comfort now. I don't go in hunger now. I say both lives I led were good, and I like both."
  —Mary Ann Sundown, a Yupik Eskimo from the Bering Sea coast

. . . hoping to preserve the unique joys and freedoms of life in "the last frontier."

"When I was a kid in Alaska, I couldn't wait until I was old enough to leave, looking for a more sophisticated way of life and a job in the Lower Forty-eight. Now I can't wait until I can retire and move back there."
  —Marilyn Curtis, born in Anchorage, living in San Francisco

"Our former governor Jay Hammond used to note: Alaska's not just a great state; it's a state of mind. We all need our dreams, and Alaska provides the fuel to keep them going."
  —Bill Perhach, bus driver in Denali National Park

Sprawling across the northwestern corner of North America, Alaska has always been a land of extremes—the farthest, biggest, coldest, and wildest place. Like all frontiers, it has attracted its share of adventurers and dreamers, loners and misfits, giving rise to the image of Alaska as a place where everyone is a rugged individualist. Now Alaska's people face the challenge of working together to steer their state into a future of social, economic, and environmental change.

1 "THE GREAT LAND"

Southeastern Alaska

When the first white people came to Alaska, they met the Aleuts. These Native people lived on a string of islands at the end of a long finger of land stretching out into the sea. To the east was the mainland, which the Aleuts called Alyeska (al-YES-ka). This old Aleut name is often said to mean "the great land."

Alaska *is* a great land, in more ways than one. "This is the Last Frontier, a land of gold rushes and bush pilots, of blue glaciers and snowy mountains, of the oil pipeline and bountiful salmon," a traveler named Matt Nauman wrote excitedly during his first visit to Alaska. He wanted to see the "real Alaska"—but he soon realized that he couldn't hope to see it all. Alaska is simply too big.

THE BIGGEST STATE

The single most important fact about Alaska, the thing that astounds every visitor and shapes the life of every resident, is the size of the place. It is one-fifth the size of the rest of the nation and two and a half times as large as Texas. Its coastline is longer than all the coastlines of the rest of the United States added together.

This state is not just big, it's also filled with big things. Alaska has the highest mountain in North America: Mount Denali, also called McKinley, which is 20,320 feet high. It has the country's largest national park, Wrangell-Saint Elias (13 million acres); its

The twin summits of massive Mount McKinley, or Denali, are the highest in North America.

largest national forest, Tongass (50,000 square miles); and its largest state park, Wood-Tikchik (1.6 million acres). Alaska has the world's longest chain of active volcanoes. It has more glaciers, or moving ice fields, than the rest of the inhabited world, and the biggest ones are larger than the state of Rhode Island. Even Alaska's natural disasters are huge. The most powerful recorded earthquake in North American history rocked central Alaska in 1964.

The second key fact about Alaska is that, like Hawaii, it is separated from the rest of the United States. Alaska is bordered on the north by the Arctic Ocean and on the south by the Gulf of Alaska and Pacific Ocean. To the west are the Bering Sea and Chukchi Sea, with Russia on the other side. At their closest point, Russia and Alaska are only fifty-one miles apart. To the east is Canada. Alaskans call the rest of the continental United States, below Canada, the Lower Forty-eight.

FIVE REGIONS

Alaska is shaped roughly like a square standing on two legs. One leg is the panhandle, which runs southeast along the coast of Canada. The other is the Alaska Peninsula, which stretches southwest and then breaks up into a sixteen-hundred-mile-long chain of islands called the Aleutians—the home of the Aleuts. The state's five geographic regions are the southeast, the south central, the southwest, the interior, and the far north.

Southeast. Alaska's southeastern panhandle is a region of water and land, a narrow strip of islands, inlets, and peninsulas. The Inside Passage is a waterway that threads among the islands, sheltering ships from the storms of the open northern sea. To the east, the Coast Mountains march along the passage in snowcapped majesty.

"This place is like a picture from a calendar or something," said tourist Martine Wirley, watching from the deck of a cruise ship as the morning fog lifted. Ahead, a ribbon of silver water wound between dozens of islands carpeted with dark green spruce and hemlock trees. "It's the most peaceful place I've ever seen."

A fishing boat trolls at the northern end of the Inside Passage, where a jumble of snow-clad peaks meets the sea.

South Central. At the top of the panhandle the Coast Range gives way to the rugged Saint Elias Mountains, marking the beginning of south-central Alaska, a region of mountains, glaciers, forests, lakes, and streams. This steep and dramatic landscape was shaped by huge ice sheets that carved deep, narrow valleys during ice ages many thousands of years ago.

The Saint Elias, Chugach, and Talkeetna Mountains follow the coast. A little inland are the Wrangell Mountains. Still farther inland sweeps the Alaska Range. Many of the mountains are volcanoes, part of the "Ring of Fire" that encircles the Pacific Ocean. These ranges also contain most of the state's twenty-nine thousand square miles of glaciers. Some glaciers cling to high mountain slopes, while others flow like sluggish rivers of ice through the valleys. The spectacular tidewater glaciers drop into the sea.

At the middle of the southern coast is the Kenai Peninsula. The Kenai Mountains run the length of the peninsula. On either side are huge, deep inlets of the sea: Prince William Sound on the east and Cook Inlet on the west.

Southwest. Southwestern Alaska begins at the long Alaska Peninsula, with the Aleutian Mountains as its backbone. These mountains seethe and hiss with volcanic life. Mount Pavlof, near the end of the peninsula, has erupted more than forty times since 1760. The biggest recorded eruption in Alaska occurred here in June of 1912, when a volcano in what is now Katmai National Park hurled so much ash into the air that skies were dark over most of the northern hemisphere for several days.

Lake Iliamna in the southwest covers 1,150 square miles and is

LAND AND WATER

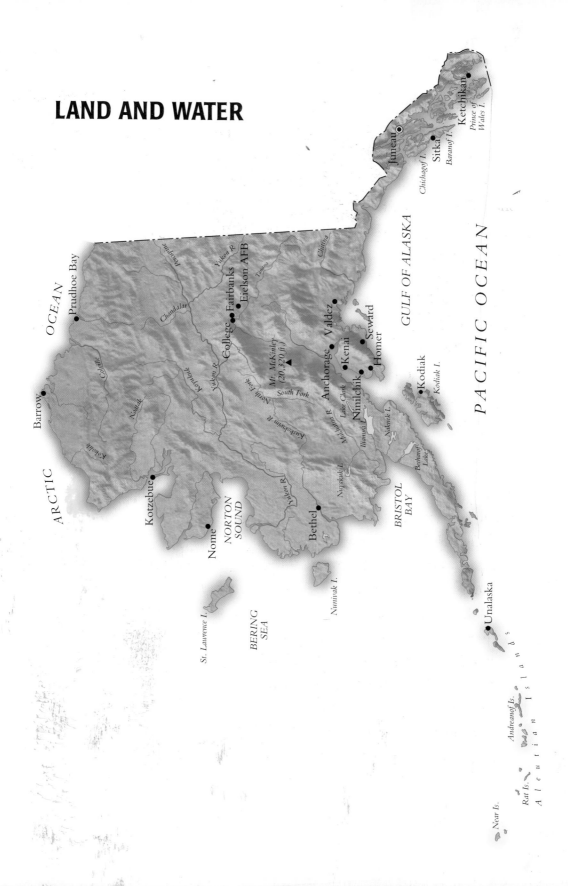

OCEAN

ARCTIC

Prudhoe Bay

Colville

Noatak

Kobuk

Barrow

Kotzebue

Nome

NORTON SOUND

BERING SEA

St. Lawrence I.

Nunivak I.

Bethel

Kuskokwim R.

Yukon R.

Koyukuk R.

Yukon R.

Chandalar

Porcupine

Yukon R.

Tanana

Fairbanks

College

Eielson AFB

Mt. McKinley
(20,320 ft.)

South Fork

North Fork

Anchorage

Valdez

Seward

Kenai

Homer

Ninilchik

Lake Clark

Iliamna

Mulchatna R.

Nushagak R.

Nuyakuk L.

Naknek L.

Becharof Lake

BRISTOL BAY

Kodiak

Kodiak I.

Chitina

GULF OF ALASKA

Juneau

Chichagof I.

Sitka

Baranof I.

Ketchikan

Prince of Wales I.

PACIFIC OCEAN

Unalaska

Aleutian Islands

Andreanof Is.

Rat Is.

Near Is.

the largest of the state's three million lakes. Kodiak Island, at 3,588 square miles, is the second-largest island in the United States, after Hawaii. Farther west are broad plains, sprinkled with lakes, where the Yukon and Kuskokwim Rivers meet the sea.

—The Aleutian Islands trail out to sea "like the tail on a kite," says Dan Grindling. These hilly, grass-covered islands are remote and not easy to reach, but they have a rugged beauty all their own. Abi Woodbridge owns a gift shop in Unalaska, the largest city in the islands. "There's something magical about this place," Woodbridge says. "When I came here in 1974, I just knew I was home."

Interior. The interior of Alaska is bordered on the south by the towering Alaska Range, where Mount Denali rises. Beyond the Alaska Range are the Kuskokwim, Kaiyuh, Ray, and White Ranges. These mountains are low and weathered, giving the land a broad, rolling appearance. The Yukon River, which flows across the interior from the Canadian border to the Yukon Delta, is the third-longest river in the United States, after the Mississippi and the Missouri. Its course cuts through a low-lying region called the Yukon Flats, covered with moist, boggy terrain called muskeg.

Far North. Alaska's far north begins with the Seward Peninsula and the Brooks Range. The Seward Peninsula is a broad, mostly treeless arm of land reaching toward Russia. The Brooks Range is a series of mountain ranges that separates Alaska's interior from the North Slope, a broad plain that runs down to the Arctic Ocean. Part of the peninsula and all of the North Slope are tundra, a generally flat landscape covered with tough mosses and hardy grasses. The only trees that grow in the tundra look more like low shrubs. Willow trees are only a few inches tall!

Fall colors blaze across the landscape near the Alaska Range.

Several feet beneath the ground's surface is permafrost, frozen soil that never thaws and cannot absorb water. During the brief northern summer, surface water forms a web of lakes and ponds across the tundra, which blazes with the brilliant colors of short-lived wildflowers. People who live here build their houses on posts. Otherwise, the warmth from the houses would melt the permafrost, turning the tundra to mud, and the houses would sink. Even with the posts, the ground under a tundra house can get soggy. Some families have to move their houses every few years.

People who make the Alaskan interior their home must learn to live with wild weather extremes!

RAIN, SNOW, AND WIND

"Alaska's almost big enough to be a continent in itself," says a weather reporter in Anchorage, in the south-central region. "We have half a dozen different climates. The south coast is as different from the north coast as Texas is from Minnesota."

Southern Alaska has a maritime climate, meaning that the sea keeps temperatures from becoming extremely hot or cold. The far north is the coldest region all year round. The interior of Alaska sees the most extreme changes in temperature. The lowest *and* highest temperatures ever recorded in Alaska came from the interior: –80 degrees Fahrenheit at Prospect Creek Camp in 1971, and 100 degrees at Fort Yukon in 1915. The people of Fairbanks, the biggest city of the interior, have learned to make the best of their harsh weather. Every March they hold an Ice Art Festival. Artists carve huge chunks of ice into dragons, mermaids, and other shapes all around town.

"To tell you about how cold it can get in Alaska," says Jerry Jacka, who used to live in Fairbanks, "one day I bought groceries and accidentally left the bananas in the car. That night the temperature dropped to 30 degrees below zero. The next morning the bananas were hard as rocks, and when I tapped them together they sounded like some sort of musical instrument. I made banana bread out of them and have had a beautiful singing voice ever since. Well, that last line is a little bit of an exaggeration, but most stories from Alaska are."

The panhandle gets a lot of rain but little snow except in the mountains. In contrast, snow blankets much of the interior during winter. The North Slope receives less, but there the biting wind molds the snow into deep drifts. High winds are an Alaskan weather hazard. Alaskans even have special names for their winds. Williwaws are sudden, unexpected gusts. Takus are bitterly cold, fast winds that rush down from ice caps high in the mountains onto southeastern communities. Chinooks are fast, warm winter winds that thaw ice and snow, destroy homes, and knock down power lines.

DAY AND NIGHT

Alaska is sometimes called the Land of the Midnight Sun. The farther north you go in summertime, the longer the days and the shorter the nights. The Arctic Circle marks the point where the sun doesn't set at all on the longest day of summer. North of the Arctic Circle, the sun stays in the sky for days at a time. In Barrow, on the north coast, the sun rises on May 10 and doesn't set until August 2, eighty-four days later. Many northern communities celebrate the midnight sun of summer. The people of Nome, for example, hold a midsummer festival that includes a softball tournament, races for rafts and mountain bikes, a barbecued-chicken feast, and a pie-eating contest.

For every long summer day, however, there comes a long winter night. During the winter, northern days get shorter and nights get longer. At the Arctic Circle, the sun doesn't rise at all on the shortest day of the year. In Barrow, the sun sets on November 18 and doesn't rise until January 24. "Land of the Midnight Sun sounds good," says Anita Rees, who lives in a cabin in the interior, "but Alaska could just as truly be called Land of the Dark Noon."

Some Alaskans suffer from cabin fever, feelings of restlessness or sadness during the long, dark winters when people spend most of their time indoors. Tempers can wear thin by spring. Governor Tony Knowles has said, "April is one tough month. Expectations rise as spring approaches, but if it stays cold or snows in April, peo-

In the Land of the Midnight Sun, the summer sun doesn't set. It dips down to the horizon and then rolls back up into the sky.

ple find that spring hasn't provided a cure-all. They go crazy." Says Harold Weaver, a newspaper editor in Anchorage, "Some people can't handle the cold and the dark. They come alive again when they can shake off their cabin fever."

"THIS GLORY OF LIGHT"

The night sky of Alaska often shimmers and glows with the eerily beautiful northern lights, or aurora borealis. In the late 1800s, the naturalist John Muir visited Alaska and was carried away by "this glory of light, so pure, so bright, so enthusiastic in motion."

The northern lights can appear as bands of color that stretch across the sky or sheets of light that ripple like immense silken curtains in the heavens. Some people say that the lights make a rustling or swishing sound but no one has been able to prove this. Electrical energy from the sun, drawn to the polar regions by the earth's magnetic field, strikes gas particles in the earth's upper atmosphere and causes them to light up.

You don't have to go to Alaska to see the northern lights. The aurora borealis appears across Canada and is sometimes seen in the northern Lower Forty-eight. But Alaskans have a much better chance of seeing it than most Americans. In Fairbanks you can see the northern lights about two hundred forty nights a year.

WILD ALASKA

Wildlife is one of Alaska's glories. The coastal waters are home to many kinds of fish, seabirds, sea otters, walruses, seals, sea lions, and whales. Sitka deer and moose live in the south. Moose also feed on the spruce, aspen, and willow forests of the interior.

Alaska has three kinds of bears: black, brown (also called grizzlies), and polar. Black bears are common in the south and in the interior. Brown bears live in nearly all parts of the state. The Kodiak is a type of large brown bear native to Kodiak Island. Polar bears, weighing up to fifteen hundred pounds when fully grown, live along the northern and northwestern coasts and have been spotted swimming as far as fifty miles from land.

"Alaskans love telling bear stories, and the wilder the better," wrote backpacker Jim Gorman after a visit to Chugach State Park near Anchorage. Most of the stories are about the brown bear, which one old-time Alaskan hunter called "a mountain of fur and teeth." Although brown bears have attacked and killed people, such attacks are very rare. "Bears don't *want* to encounter people," says a wildlife biologist. "If a bear hears you coming, he'll get out of your way."

In wilderness areas, the song of the wolf floats through the Alaskan night. Wolves prey on young or sick deer and other large mammals, but most of the time they live on small creatures such as lemmings, the mouselike rodents of the tundra.

Caribou roam the northern tundra in huge herds that may total two hundred thousand animals. Each winter they cross the Brooks Range to spend the cold months foraging for food in the interior. Musk oxen, shaggy-haired wild cattle, lived in the far north until hunters killed the last ones in 1865. Later, people brought musk oxen from Greenland to start new populations in northwestern Alaska.

At least 430 kinds of birds have been sighted in Alaska. Some of them, such as ravens, bald eagles, ptarmigans, and snowy owls, live there all year long. Others spend only the spring and summer months in Alaska, feeding and breeding and raising their young. Uncountable millions of ducks, geese, and waterbirds migrate annually to Alaska's lakes and marshes from all over the world. The Arctic tern makes the longest journey of any bird: a 22,000-mile round trip each year between Alaska and Antarctica.

The grizzly bear is majestic and the wolf is wily, but Alaska's most feared wild creature may just be the mosquito. Enormous swarms of

These playful polar bears are powerful and dangerous hunters.

The moose, almost always grazing, is a common sight in southern and central Alaska.

mosquitoes hatch in pools all over the state every summer. Stinging and humming, thick clouds of these insects have been known to drive caribou into rivers and people into hysterics.

WHERE THE PEOPLE ARE

People and the things they build are part of the Alaskan landscape. With an area of 587,878 square miles and a population estimated at 587,000 in 1995, Alaska has about one person for every square mile in the state. Compare this with 70 people per square mile in the United States as a whole, or 333 per square mile in New York State, and you'll see that Alaska is very thinly populated.

There are thousands of square miles where nobody lives. The 1994 *Alaska Almanac* estimates that only 160,000 of Alaska's 365 million land acres show signs of human use. In other words, people have changed only about one-twentieth of one percent of the land.

The greatest concentration of people—and of their cities, villages, and roads—is along the southern coast. More than half of all Alaskans live in or near Anchorage. At the other end of the scale are tiny communities such as Red Devil, a town on the Kusko-kwim River, which has forty-seven inhabitants.

LIVING WITH WILDERNESS

Two-thirds of Alaska, or about 387,000 square miles, is federal land. Some of this land is set aside for military bases. Enormous tracts of it, especially in the southwest, west, and northeast, are national wildlife refuges. The rest of the public land is controlled by the Bureau of Land Management, the National Forest Service, or the National Park Service.

Although many people live on these public lands, and private landholdings are scattered through them, the U.S. government is the state's biggest landowner. "Alaska is kind of weird that way," says Scott Fierabend, who works for the National Wildlife Federation in Anchorage. "Since most of it is federal land, the state's major policy issues are going to be decided by the Lower Forty-eight." This makes some Alaskans bitter. One told a reporter,

Most settlements are along the coast. Here in Ketchikan, inlets and canals form streets for kayakers.

"What bugs me is that when decisions are made about Alaska, people from Texas and Ohio, California and New York carry more weight than people from Alaska."

The land and its resources are the subject of many conflicts. On one side are those who want to protect the land and its creatures so that the wilderness will be there for future generations. On the other are those who believe that it is better to use resources such as timber, oil, and minerals to create jobs and profits now. The federal government is trying to balance the views of environmentalists and developers.

Two battles concern the Tongass National Forest in the southeast and the Arctic National Wildlife Refuge in the far north. Although a 1990 law protects the Tongass, Congress has searched for ways to allow increased logging there. And pressure is increasing to drill for oil in the Arctic refuge, although biologists say that drilling will damage the fragile tundra environment and hurt the caribou herds.

People who live and work in Alaska's public lands often resent the rules they must follow. Residents of the small settlement of Chisana, in the Wrangell-Saint Elias National Preserve, met with Park Service workers to air their complaints. They grumbled about limits on hunting and about the permits they had to get before they could put up new buildings.

One resident told a park worker, "Because of all the demands you people make, soon there will be nobody here, just the way you want it." Another man, who arranges trips for hunters and other visitors, said, "You call this public land, but pretty soon nobody will be able to use it but the Park Service."

A Park Service official had a different view. "Wilderness is disappearing faster than people think," he said. "Wrangell-Saint Elias is a treasure worth preserving, a large intact ecosystem rarely found anymore. We see ourselves as bankers, saving it for the future." Fred Ewan, an elderly Native whose people have lived in the region for thousands of years, agreed. "It's good they made the park," he told a reporter. "Good for the animals. There were too many people shooting them."

Only a few determined travelers make it all the way north to the rugged Brooks Range, the gateway to the Arctic.

Cordova Bay, Prince William Sound, *by William Keith*

The first people in the Americas came from Asia, and the first place they set foot was Alaska. They crossed the Bering Sea on a land bridge that appeared during the ice ages, when much of the earth's water was frozen and its seas were shallower.

Scientists believe that bands of hunters crossed from Siberia to North America between forty thousand and fifteen thousand years ago. These wanderers gradually spread outward to become the ancestors of all the original peoples of North and South America. Around twelve thousand years ago the ice melted and the waters rose, covering the land bridge. By that time, however, the people of the far north could cross the Bering Strait by boat.

THE FIRST ALASKANS

The Native people of Alaska formed many different cultures. These cultures fell into three main groups: the Indians, the Aleuts, and the Eskimos, who are sometimes called the Inuit. When Europeans first encountered the Alaskans in the mid-1700s, each group lived in a separate area and did not mingle with the others. All lived by hunting, fishing, and gathering wild foods such as berries and roots.

The Indians. The Tlingit and Haida Indians lived in the southeast. They had moved there from what is now Canada and were

The Tlingit built large, sturdy houses of cedar or spruce planks. Several related families lived in each house.

closely related to other Native peoples along the coast of British Columbia. The Tlingit were traders, and the Haida were noted for making fine tools and art objects of wood, stone, bone, and shell. Both were skilled woodworkers who made dugout canoes and carved totem poles—cedar logs that served as records of their legends and histories.

The Athabascans roamed Alaska's vast interior, forcing a living from the harsh land and sometimes battling famine or starvation. They did not build permanent settlements but traveled from place to place, following game such as caribou and moose. They used snowshoes to hunt during the winter. Some Athabascans lived on the coast around Cook Inlet; salmon was a major part of their diet.

The Aleuts. The Aleuts occupied the end of the Alaska Peninsula and the Aleutian Islands. They lived in large houses in permanent villages, with as many as forty families sharing one house. In sturdy skin-covered canoes called *baidarkas*, the Aleuts skillfully navigated the dangerous, foggy seas around their islands. They used needles made from the bones of seagulls to decorate their clothing with fine embroidery.

The Eskimos. The Eskimos settled all across the northern

Aleuts near Unalaska in the Aleutian Islands. Early European visitors were amazed to see men in such low, lightweight boats hunting seals, walruses, and even small whales.

An Eskimo village, painted about 1866

coastline of North America, from the Bering Sea through Canada to Greenland. In Alaska, they lived on Kodiak Island and the upper Alaska Peninsula, on the west coast, and across the far north.

The Eskimos were probably the last group to cross over from Asia, and they were closely related to peoples on the Siberian coast. The Eskimos lived in houses called *barabaras*, which were made of thick pieces of sod on a framework of driftwood or whale bones. They gathered berries, hunted moose and caribou, and fished for salmon, but sea mammals—whales, seals, and walruses—were their major sources of food, skins, and oil for lamps. Today some Eskimos still hunt as their ancestors did. Every June they celebrate their hunting traditions at the Nalukataq Whaling Festival in Barrow, on the north coast.

RUSSIAN ALASKA

In the 1500s, European Russians looked eastward and began exploring and colonizing Siberia. Slowly they moved toward Asia's

THE GREAT RAVEN BRINGS LIFE

Ravens are clever, shiny black birds, much like crows but larger. They live nearly everywhere in Alaska. According to the Natives of Alaska, all animals and birds have spirits. The raven spirit is especially important in the religion of many Native peoples. Raven has many faces. Sometimes he is a generous giver of gifts, and sometimes he is a trickster or prankster.

The Bering Sea Eskimos tell many stories about the Great Raven, who created the world. Life began when Raven dropped peas onto the ground. Each pea turned into a man. Raven then made animals out of clay: two bears, two wolves, two squirrels, and so on until he had created all the animals. Finally he took more clay and made a woman, the wife of the first man. That is how animals and people came into the world.

Pacific coast. Czar Peter the Great sent Vitus Bering, a Danish officer serving in the Russian navy, to see whether Siberia and North America were joined by land. In 1728, Bering sailed north through the strait that now bears his name, proving that Asia and the Americas were not connected. But he didn't see America, which was hidden by fog. In 1741 he tried again to locate the north-western coast of America, and this time he succeeded.

Bering's men were the first Europeans to explore in depth the sea that bears his name. They went ashore on Kayak Island, off Alaska's south coast. There Georg Steller, a German naturalist who sailed with Bering, found what he called "signs of people and their doings": cut trees and bones, dried salmon, and ropes made of seaweed.

Bering's men carried sea-otter skins back to Russia, where the soft, silky furs caused a sensation. Soon Russian traders and adventurers were heading to the Aleutian Islands for furs, which fetched high prices in Europe and China. By the end of the 1700s, the sea otter was almost extinct. Tragically, the Russians nearly wiped out the Aleuts as well. The Europeans introduced deadly diseases such as smallpox and tuberculosis. They also enslaved the Aleuts and treated them brutally. In 1762, when the Aleuts rebelled against this treatment, the Russians killed thousands of them.

The Russians built their first permanent base in Alaska in 1784, on Kodiak Island. Under their influence, many Natives there learned to speak Russian and adopted the Russian Orthodox

Vitus Bering's second expedition reached the shores of Alaska. But Bering died before he could return to Russia with news of his discovery.

religion, a form of Christianity. The Russian influence lingers on in Kodiak today. Every January, islanders follow the Russian Orthodox tradition of "starring." Led by someone twirling a large star, a choir visits church members' homes to sing hymns. Russian food is served at a big New Year's dinner in the church, after which everyone puts on masks for a costume ball.

In 1799, Czar Paul I put a fur-trading firm called the Russian-American Company in charge of all Russian operations in Alaska. The company sent Aleksandr Baranov, a merchant from Siberia, to manage the colony. Baranov made his headquarters near the present-day site of Sitka, in the southeast. The local Tlingit fiercely resisted the Russian invasion, but by 1804 Baranov and his men, along with their Aleut slaves, had won control of the area.

American writer Washington Irving called Baranov "a rough, rugged, hospitable, hard-drinking, old Russian, somewhat of a soldier, somewhat of a trader." Under Baranov's leadership, the fur trade prospered and Sitka flourished. After Baranov retired in 1818, Sitka continued to grow. Although tales of Sitka as the glamorous "Paris of the North" are exaggerated, the city had a school, library, hospital, and cathedral.

THE UNITED STATES TAKES OVER

By 1867, Russia was busy with European affairs and was losing control of its American colony. The British and the Americans were poised to move in. To keep the British out, Russia offered to sell Alaska to the United States. Secretary of State William Seward wanted his country to acquire this huge territory and its resources

One historian called Aleksandr Baranov "a man of iron energy and nerve." Baranov ruled Russian Alaska for almost twenty years.

Baranov and his men built a fort at Sitka, which soon became the bustling trade center of the far north.

of minerals, timber, and fish. He arranged for the United States to buy Alaska for $7.2 million, or two cents an acre.

Seward knew that he had made one of the greatest real-estate bargains in history. "But," he said, "it will take the people a generation to find out." Many Americans criticized the purchase, calling Alaska "Seward's Folly." They thought the place was an icy wasteland and couldn't imagine why anyone would want it. They soon found out.

In 1880, two prospectors named Joe Juneau and Richard Harris found gold in southeastern Alaska. Within a short time, hundreds of gold hunters had flocked to the site. They founded the town of

At this ceremony on October 18, 1867, Russia signed over Alaska to the United States. Some disgusted Americans called their new territory "the polar bear garden."

Miners dream of Yukon gold, as they struggle up the Chilkoot Pass in 1898.

Juneau, which later became Alaska's capital. A much larger gold rush started in 1896, when prospectors found gold in the Klondike, a region in Canada's Yukon Territory. Southern Alaska was the gateway to the Klondike, and by the following year thousands of hopeful gold seekers from all over the world thronged the muddy streets of the tiny town of Skagway, waiting for their turn to clamber up the steep, dangerous Chilkoot Pass into the Yukon.

The next year, people found gold on the beaches of Nome, kick-

THE KLONDIKE GOLD RUSH

Gold was discovered in Forty Mile Creek in the Yukon Territory in 1887 and over the border on the Canadian side at Klondike in 1896. The term Klondike was loosely used for both the Alaskan and Canadian diggings. The gold rush to the rugged, frozen North rivaled anything that had been experienced in the Lower Forty-eight.

A POET IN THE GOLD RUSH

Writer and poet Hamlin Garland left his home in Wisconsin to join the 1898 gold rush. He wasn't looking for gold. He wrote, "I believed that I was about to see and take part in a most picturesque and impressive movement across the wilderness. I believed it to be the last great march of the kind which could ever come in America, so rapidly were the wild places being filled up." Garland recorded his wilderness experience in poems such as "Do You Fear the Wind?" from his book *The Trail of the Goldseekers*.

Do you fear the force of the wind,
The slash of the rain?
Go and face them and fight them,
Be savage again.
Go hungry and cold like the wolf,
Go wade like the crane:
The palms of your hands will thicken,
The skin of your cheek will tan,
You'll grow ragged and weary and swarthy
But you'll walk like a man.

ing off the biggest and wildest gold rush in American history. By the summer of 1900, more than 230 ships had brought eighteen thousand prospectors to western Alaska. Tents sprang up everywhere. Gold seekers who didn't have tents slept on the sand. In the scramble for riches, some resorted to theft and even murder. People still travel to Nome every summer to camp on the beaches and search for gold—but their camps are a lot less rowdy than those of the old-time prospectors!

The lawless gold rushes made some Americans think that

Alaska needed a dose of law and order. Samuel Hall Young agreed. He was a preacher who went to Alaska in 1878 and took part in the gold rushes as a missionary. Young criticized the federal government for neglecting Alaska. He wrote, "The struggle of Alaskans for their rights as American citizens forms one of the gloomy pages of American history."

The army, the customs office, and the navy had each tried to govern Alaska since 1867, with little success. In 1884, the U.S. Congress named it a district of the United States and tried to establish order by extending Oregon's laws northward. In 1912, Alaska was made a territory, with a governor and an elected legislature, or lawmaking body. Alaskans had been allowed to send a representative to Congress for six years now, but he still had no vote.

TWENTIETH-CENTURY CHANGES

In 1914, the federal government began building a railroad to connect the harbors of Alaska's south coast with the mines and coalfields of the interior. By this time, most gold and copper mining in Alaska was done by large companies that could afford the equipment for underground operations. The salmon-fishing industry was well established along the south coast, with dozens of canneries preparing fish for shipment to other parts of the world. Lumber companies were beginning to harvest the mighty, ancient forests of southern Alaska—the first wood-pulp mill opened near Juneau in 1922. The Great Depression, which plunged much of the world into economic chaos in the 1930s, had little effect on Alaska because gold continued to sell at a high price.

President Warren G. Harding, the first president to visit Alaska, drives the spike completing the Alaska Railroad in 1923.

For years, many people in the Lower Forty-eight hardly thought about Alaska. In 1941, however, Japan bombed a U.S. naval base in Hawaii, and the United States declared war on Japan. Americans suddenly realized that part of their nation—the western islands of Alaska—was closer to Japan than to Washington, D.C. Japanese bombers attacked a naval base in the Aleutian Islands in 1942, and Japanese troops seized the islands of Attu and Kiska. The United States acted quickly, sending about two hundred thousand soldiers to Alaska. After fighting the Aleutian Campaign, called the Thousand Mile War, they recaptured Attu and Kiska in 1943.

When the war began, Alaska could be reached only by ship or airplane. The U.S. government needed a land route for supplies and equipment to support the war effort, and in 1942, with permission from Canada, it created one. In just eight months, in one of the greatest engineering feats of modern times, the Army Corps of Engineers built the first road linking Alaska with the Lower Forty-eight. It ran for 1,520 miles from Dawson in British Columbia through the Yukon Territory to Fairbanks. Sometimes called the Alcan Highway, the Alaska Highway is still the only road into Alaska.

World War II changed Alaska in several ways. It gave the territory

POPULATION GROWTH: 1880–1990

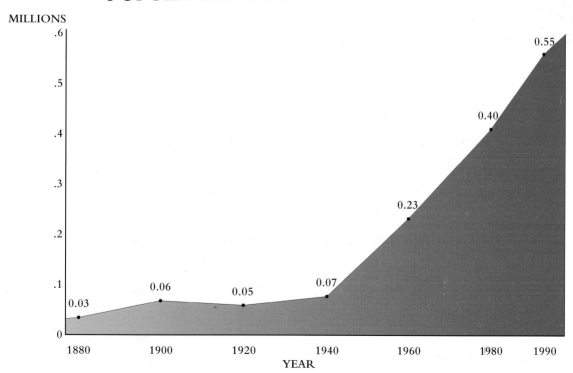

a highway *and* thousands of new residents, people who went to Alaska on military service or as workers on military construction sites and settled there. For a long time, Alaskans had been asking Congress to make their territory into a state. Now, with the surge in population, demands for statehood grew louder.

Alaskans believed that they could demonstrate that they were ready for statehood by preparing a state constitution. In 1955 they chose delegates from all over the territory to draw one up. The delegates created a document that the National Municipal League called "one of the best, if not the best, state constitutions ever written." Alaska's voters approved the constitution in 1956, and Congress passed the Alaska Statehood Act. Alaska became the forty-ninth state of the Union on January 3, 1959.

THE RUSH FOR LIQUID GOLD

Soon the new state experienced a different kind of gold rush—a rush for petroleum, or "liquid gold." Pumps in the Kenai Peninsula had been bringing up oil since the 1950s. In 1968 geologists discovered a larger reserve at Prudhoe Bay, on the North Slope. There was just one problem with this discovery: How would the oil get from the Arctic to world markets?

Petroleum companies wanted to build a pipeline to carry the oil and natural gas through Alaska to a port on the south coast. Environmentalists protested. If the pipeline sprang a leak, the spill could harm wilderness and wildlife. Natives whose traditional lands lay along the pipeline route also protested. Nevertheless, the federal government allowed a group of oil companies to build the

Trans-Alaska Pipeline. The pipeline runs for eight hundred miles, from Prudhoe Bay to the port of Valdez (val-DEEZ), across eight hundred rivers and streams and through three mountain ranges.

The accident that environmentalists had feared didn't come from the pipeline. It came in March of 1989, when the Exxon oil tanker *Valdez* ran onto a reef of rock in Prince William Sound and spilled eleven million gallons of oil into what were once crystal-clear waters. The spill was the worst ecological disaster the world had seen. Wind and tides smeared hundreds of miles of coastline with

Oil begins its 800-mile journey through the Trans-Alaska Pipeline here at Prudhoe Bay in the Arctic.

Volunteers from many states joined cleanup crews after a massive oil spill in Prince William Sound in 1989.

sticky oil. Untold numbers of seabirds and mammals perished, coated with oil. Commercial fisheries in the area closed; some remain closed today. A federal jury found the Exxon Corporation and the captain of the *Valdez* guilty of recklessness, and Exxon has been ordered to pay billions of dollars for the damage caused by the spill.

Some people believe that the 1989 spill caused less harm than was first feared. "No one wants to know what the truth is. No one wants to know the science behind it," says Jeff Wheelwright, author of *Degrees of Disaster*, who thinks that Prince William Sound has recovered. Most scientists, however, believe that the long-term effects of the spill won't be known for many years.

Oil's other effects on Alaska are easier to see. Throughout the 1970s and early 1980s, people flocked to Alaska to work on the pipeline and in the petroleum industry. The state's population increased by almost one-third during the 1970s. The oil boom boosted incomes and gave the state money for dozens of new roads, schools, airstrips, and other construction projects in many parts of the state. Then world oil prices dropped in 1985, and Alaska's oil production and income dropped, too. Oil and natural gas are still very important to the economy, but the "gold rush" days are over.

3 LAWS AND LIVELIHOOD

State capitol in Juneau

Alaskans are very interested in politics. Political events touch their lives daily, especially because the state and federal governments control most of the land and many of the jobs in Alaska.

INSIDE GOVERNMENT

Alaska's state government is modeled on the federal government. It has three branches: the executive, the legislative, and the judicial.

Executive. The executive branch carries out the state's laws. The head of the executive branch is the governor, who is assisted by the lieutenant governor. Alaskans elect their governor and lieutenant governor every four years. No governor can serve more than two four-year terms in a row.

The governor of Alaska is one of the most powerful in the United States. He appoints all of the state's top officials, including the attorney general, all district attorneys, and the judges, and runs the fifteen major departments of the state government, including Community and Regional Affairs, Education, Health and Social Services, Labor, Natural Resources, and Transportation.

Legislative. The legislative branch of government, called the state legislature, makes the state's laws and approves the budget, which says how the state's money will be spent (although the governor can change items in the budget). The state legislature has

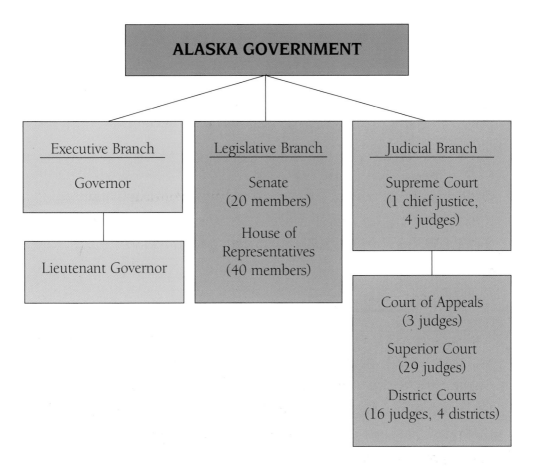

ALASKA GOVERNMENT

Executive Branch

Governor

Lieutenant Governor

Legislative Branch

Senate
(20 members)

House of
Representatives
(40 members)

Judicial Branch

Supreme Court
(1 chief justice,
4 judges)

Court of Appeals
(3 judges)

Superior Court
(29 judges)

District Courts
(16 judges, 4 districts)

two houses, a senate and a house of representatives. Voters elect twenty senators for four-year terms and forty representatives for two-year terms. To vote, residents must be at least eighteen years old and must have lived in Alaska for at least a year. Alaska also sends two senators and one representative to the U.S. Congress.

Unlike the rest of the states, Alaska has not been divided into counties and townships. About two-thirds of the state has no organized local government because the population is so small and spread out. The state legislature governs this unorganized territory.

Judicial. The judicial branch upholds the law through the court system. Alaska has four levels of courts. District courts handle minor civil and criminal cases. They also issue marriage licenses. Someone who disagrees with the verdict of a district court can appeal it, or ask for the case to be retried in a higher court.

The next level is superior court, where more serious civil and criminal cases are tried. All cases that involve children and minors are heard in a superior court. The appeals court, consisting of three judges, hears appeals from the district and superior courts. The state's highest court is the five-member supreme court. It has the final say on all appeals from the lower courts.

ALASKAN ISSUES

Modern Alaska was shaped by two important acts of the U.S. Congress. In 1971, responding to claims by Native Alaskans that they had been unfairly stripped of rights to their traditional lands, Congress passed the Alaska Native Land Claims Settlement Act (ANLCSA). The act gave Eskimos, Aleuts, and Indians $925 million and title to 40 million acres of land. The federal government also created thirteen regional Native corporations and several hundred village corporations to manage the money and land that the Natives received under the settlement.

In 1980, Congress passed a bill that more than doubled the amount of federal land in Alaska. The Alaska Lands Act added 54 billion acres to the national wildlife refuge system, 44 million acres to the national park system, and 3 million acres to the national forest system, as well as adding parts of 25 rivers to the national wild and scenic river system. Lovers of wilderness rejoiced. Many

BENNY BENSON'S FLAG

Alaska's state flag was created decades before Alaska became a state. In 1926 the Territory of Alaska held a contest for schoolchildren to design a territorial flag. Benny Benson, a thirteen-year-old Aleut seventh grader, turned in the winning entry.

Benny Benson's design was a blue background with eight gold stars: the North Star and the constellation that some call the Big Dipper and others the Great Bear. Said Benny, "The blue field is for the Alaska sky and the forget-me-not, an Alaska flower. The North Star is for the future state of Alaska, the most northerly of the Union. The Great Bear—symbolizing strength." His flag flew over the Territory of Alaska until 1959, when Alaska became a state. On July 4, 1959, when the flag was raised in the new state capital for the first time, Benny Benson led a parade carrying his flag.

Alaskans, however, complained that too much of their state had been removed from local control. In both Alaska and Washington, D.C., people continue to debate the future of these lands.

Alaskan politics can be very complicated. Many federal, state, and local agencies, boards, and officials may be involved in a single decision. Buying land is a good example of how Alaska is different from other states. The easiest way to get land is to buy it from someone who already owns it. Less than 1 percent of the land, however, belongs to private owners. Most of this land is located in towns or along roads. Because it is easy to reach, it is considered the most desirable land in the state—and its price goes steadily up.

Federal homesteading programs, which gave free land to anyone willing to settle and work on it, ended in Alaska in 1986. The state allows people to homestead on state-owned land, but they must build a house and meet other requirements. "It isn't easy to get land here," says a woman who moved to Alaska with her husband, seven children, and twenty goats in 1974, "but it's possible."

ALASKA'S ECONOMY

Alaska's economy depends largely on natural resources, which means that it is a "boom and bust" economy. When world prices for Alaska's resources are high, the state prospers. When prices drop, the state suffers. Alaska is trying to create a more balanced economy by developing manufacturing industries. The number of service jobs—including jobs in education, health care, entertainment, and tourism—is also growing. Still, unemployment is a nagging problem. Some people cannot find jobs, and some jobs last

Akutan, in the Aleutian Islands. For some Alaskans, home is a small village or an isolated homestead.

for just one season. Industries such as fishing and tourism hire workers in summer and lay them off in winter.

Although only about 4 percent of Alaskans work in the petroleum industry, oil is vital to the state's economy. Oil companies pay state taxes on the oil and gas they drill on the Kenai Peninsula and the North Slope, and Alaska also receives a share of the money the companies make when they sell the oil. About eighty-five cents of every dollar of state money comes from oil. Alaska has lead, coal, zinc, gold, silver, platinum, and tin mines. Some scientists think that large reserves of coal and other resources remain to be discovered under the Alaskan soil.

Commercial farming is centered in the valleys of the Tanana and Matanuska Rivers. The major crops are hay (for feeding livestock), potatoes, barley, oats, and vegetables. Long summer days and mild temperatures produce Alaska's famous giant vegetables, such as ninety-pound cabbages.

Winter sea ice surrounds an oil-drilling platform in Cook Inlet.

ka salmon. Others, however, point out that the price of salmon on the world market has gone up and down many times.

The government is the biggest employer in Alaska. About 29 percent of the work force is employed directly by the federal, state, or local government. In addition, many jobs in the construction industry come from government projects.

Tourism was launched in Alaska in the 1890s when passenger ships began cruising the Inside Passage. Today more than one million people visit Alaska each year, three-quarters of them in the summertime. Although people have come to Alaska from just about every country on earth, most tourists are from other parts

A school bus serves as a shuttle for summer visitors to Denali National Park. More than one million people visit Alaska every year.

Salmon fishermen in Prince William Sound

Alaska's commercial fisheries produce more seafood than any other state. But this business, like the oil industry, has busts as well as booms. "I'm on the verge of collapse," said salmon fisherman Ross Mullins of Cordova in 1994. "And in my mind, and the minds of most fishermen down here, there's no question what the causal fact is." Mullins and many other fishermen in Prince William Sound blamed the 1989 Exxon oil spill for a disastrous slump in salmon prices, saying that the spill made people afraid to eat Alas-

SIX STATE FAIRS

Alaska is so big that it needs more than one state fair. It has six. Every year state fairs are held in Palmer, in the Matanuska Valley; in Fairbanks; in Ninilchik, on the Kenai Peninsula; in Haines, in the southeast; in Kodiak; and in Delta Junction. Only the Palmer and Fairbanks fairs are recognized by the state as "official" state fairs, but all of them offer a good time to residents and visitors.

"The best part of a fair is that it's fun," says Deidra Berberich, one of the managers of the Palmer fair. "It's a great atmosphere. The kids are jumping with excitement. Everyone shows up in a good mood. And when they leave, they're tired, but you can tell they had a good time." Palmer's festival honors the Matanuska Valley's history as Alaska's prime farmland with livestock and vegetable shows. It also features Native events, such as the Alutiiq dancers from Kodiak, and contests, such as wood splitting and water hauling.

of the United States or from Japan. They fish, hike, camp, buy souvenirs, sightsee in Denali National Park, and "flightsee" over more remote regions such as Wrangell-Saint Elias National Park, the Yukon Flats, and the Arctic tundra.

Each year tourists spend more than half a billion dollars in Alaska. More than twenty-five hundred businesses depend on sales to visitors, and tourism affects almost forty thousand of the state's jobs. Income from oil is expected to dwindle in the coming years, and the state will certainly look to tourism to help replace that money.

Some seventy thousand Alaskans, mostly Natives, follow a way of life called subsistence. They live off the land, hunting, fishing, and farming, and they produce as much of their own food, clothing, and other goods as possible. When they need money to buy something they can't make, they earn a few dollars by panning for gold or trapping for furs to sell.

A number of Alaskans still practice small-time mining. One man spends his summers with his wife and daughter in a small wooden cabin north of the Wrangell Mountains. He works a gold claim on Bonanza Creek and splits his finds with the owner of the claim, who lives in Anchorage. "An ounce of gold is a good day for us," the miner says. "It's not much money for all the hardship, but I consider it a privilege to be out here." Says his fourteen-year-old daughter, "Mom says this experience will make a better person of me."

Few people can adopt the subsistence way of life, but even those with steady jobs may boost their incomes with a little trapping or gold panning. A great many residents grow their own vegetables,

An Eskimo woman ice-fishes near Nome. Thousands of Native Alaskans practice traditional ways of living off the land.

People still pan for gold. Some earn enough to keep going but very few will ever strike it rich.

EARNING A LIVING

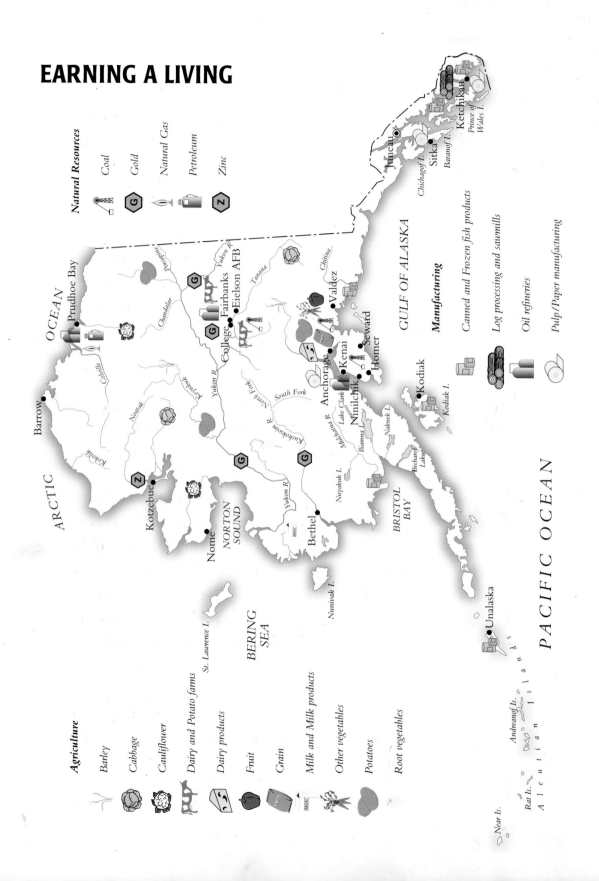

Natural Resources

- Coal
- G Gold
- Natural Gas
- Petroleum
- Z Zinc

Manufacturing

- Canned and Frozen fish products
- Log processing and sawmills
- Oil refineries
- Pulp/Paper manufacturing

Agriculture

- Barley
- Cabbage
- Cauliflower
- Dairy and Potato farms
- Dairy products
- Fruit
- Grain
- Milk and Milk products
- Other vegetables
- Potatoes
- Root vegetables

ARCTIC OCEAN

BERING SEA

GULF OF ALASKA

PACIFIC OCEAN

NORTON SOUND

BRISTOL BAY

Aleutian Islands

Near Is.
Rat Is.
Andreanof Is.

St. Lawrence I.
Nunivak I.
Kodiak I.
Chichagof I.
Baranof I.
Prince of Wales I.

Barrow
Prudhoe Bay
Kotzebue
Nome
Bethel
Unalaska
Kodiak
Homer
Seward
Kenai
Ninilchik
Anchorage
Valdez
College
Fairbanks
Eielson AFB
Juneau
Sitka
Ketchikan

Colville
Chandalar
Porcupine
Yukon R.
Tanana
Chitina
Noatak
Kobuk
Kokolik
Koyukuk
North Fork
South Fork
Kuskokwim R.
Mulchatna R.
Naknek L.
Iliamna L.
Becharof Lake
Nuyakuk L.
Lake Clark
Kvichak

Niyakuk L.

and they stock their freezers with meat they've hunted, fish they've caught, and berries they've picked. Modern Alaskans still have something in common with the first Alaskans, who lived off the land.

THE COST OF LIVING

In some ways, Alaskans pride themselves on being set apart from the rest of the country. Many of them moved to this state in search of independence, even isolation. At the same time, they pay a price for the remoteness of their home.

Things made in the Lower Forty-eight—everything from cars to comic books—cost more in Alaska because they have to be shipped so far. Travel is expensive, too. "It takes a major investment to visit the lower states, or anywhere else, for that matter," says Nancy Carlson, who lives with her large family in the interior.

The cost of living is high, but so is the average Alaskan's income. In the mid-1990s, the state was ranked eighth in the nation in average income per person. One source of money that everyone counts on is the Permanent Fund dividend. The state set up the fund to invest money so that when the North Slope oil fields run dry around the year 2015, there will be a source of income to replace them. Every year, Alaska gives part of the interest on that investment fund to people who have lived in the state for at least one full year. In 1996, each qualified resident received a check for $1,130.86.

In the mid-1990s, about 10 percent of Alaska's population lived below the poverty level, compared with 14.5 percent for the country as a whole. More of Alaska's poor live in rural areas than in the cities, but poverty and homelessness are growing problems for Anchorage and other population centers.

Twenty-five-year-old Dan Goodell was born in Alaska and lives in Anchorage. Goodell works in a restaurant during the winter and a fish cannery during the summer. He sums up the feelings of many Alaskans when he says, "A lot of people in the Lower Forty-eight dream of coming up here to live. They have this fantasy that Alaska is some kind of frontier wonderland. It *is* a wonderful place—if you've got some money. But there are a lot of people here looking for work. If you're not making it down south, Alaska isn't the answer to your problems."

GROSS STATE PRODUCT: $32 BILLION

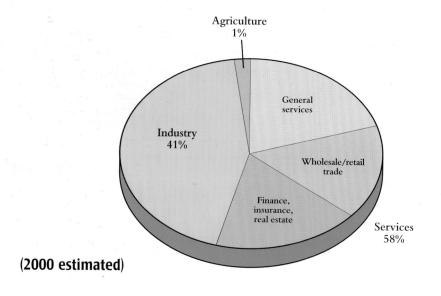

Agriculture 1%

General services

Industry 41%

Wholesale/retail trade

Finance, insurance, real estate

Services 58%

(2000 estimated)

A hunter takes aim in the twilight. Hunting and fishing are part of everyday life for many Alaskans.

4 LIFE IN THE BIG BEYOND

"The first few years I lived here I thought of Alaska as 'the Big Beyond,' " says sixty-eight-year-old Edna Laurie, who grew up in Iowa and has lived in Alaska since she was twenty-four. "When my husband said he wanted to move up here, I couldn't believe my ears. It seemed like moving to the moon. But now it's home."

Alaska is home to more people every year. Between 1980 and 1990, the state's population increased by 37 percent. (The growth was 10 percent for the entire United States.) The flow of people slowed a bit in the mid-1980s, when oil prices fell and the state's prosperity dimmed. Still, experts who study population patterns believe that Alaska's population will keep growing faster than that of the nation as a whole. Some people are drawn to Alaska by magnificent scenery. Some want to live a rugged outdoor life. Others dream of landing a good job or opening their own business.

Although all major ethnic groups are represented among the people of Alaska, the percentage of African, Hispanic, and Asian Americans is lower there than in many parts of the United States. The largest ethnic minority is Native American.

NATIVE ALASKA

Natives make up 16 percent of Alaska's population, and about half of these are Eskimos. One-fifth of Alaska's Natives live in

ETHNIC ALASKA

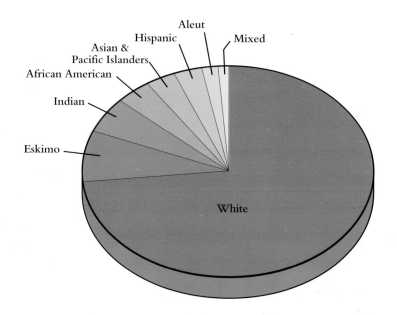

Eskimo

Indian

African American

Asian & Pacific Islanders

Hispanic

Aleut

Mixed

White

Anchorage or Fairbanks. The rest live in smaller communities scattered along the coast and rivers. In western and northern Alaska, and in parts of the interior, the majority of the population is Native.

Life changed forever for these peoples when the Europeans came. Mary Ann Sundown lived through the years of change. She was born into a traditional Eskimo community of the Yupik people near Scammon Bay, on the Bering Sea coast. Mary Ann grew up in a sod house with a single window of dried seal gut and a lamp that burned seal oil for light. She didn't see a white person until she was fifteen years old. Today her grandchildren ride snowmobiles and read fashion magazines.

Fred Ewan of the Ahtna, an Athabascan group in southern Alaska, also remembers the old ways. "We ate moose, caribou,

The Chilkat Dancers of Haines keep alive the art of making masks.

sheep, ducks, and swans. Also berries, the roots of wild rhubarb, and wild onion. We caught salmon in fish traps made from spruce branches the size of your thumb. Now," he says, "the young people eat white man's food."

Alaska's Natives lost many ties to their old ways during the 1800s and the first half of the 1900s. Missionaries and government officials tried to stamp out their languages, customs, and beliefs because they thought that the best thing for the Natives was to make them as much like white people as possible. Yet Natives were not fully accepted as equals in white society. As a result, many of them felt that they lived in two worlds but didn't truly belong to either. Some struggled with alcoholism and depression.

"Many of us are unskilled, uneducated, and lost in the predominant [white] culture," Roy Huhndorf, head of the Cook Inlet Region Native Corporation, said in 1988. "Alaska Natives exist in a time warp, and we've been victimized by it. Why do you suppose that we have such a high degree of alcoholism, drug addiction, suicide? I think cultural dislocation is the culprit."

Yet things have begun to get better since the Alaska Native Land Claims Settlement Act of 1971. The Native corporations created by the act have invested the money it awarded to Natives. These corporations now own and operate many businesses, from sawmills to hotels to computer-manufacturing companies. Natives are also taking a growing part in state and local government. To deal with alcohol abuse, some Native communities have outlawed alcohol.

And young Natives are once again learning the traditions, arts, customs, and languages of their ancestors. Mary Ann Sundown's grandchildren learn the Yupik language in school, get together with friends to perform traditional Yupik dances, and learn traditional hunting methods from their father. Her daughter says, "I want them to learn other ways—outside ways. And I want them to learn our way, too, hunting for our kind of foods. We can't have store-bought food all the time. I want them to learn both ways."

The pull of the outside world is strong for many young Natives, and most elders know that it would not be possible to return

A TASTE OF ALASKA

For thousands of years, the firm, pink flesh of the salmon has been an important food source for many of Alaska's Natives. But these nutritious fish are not available all year round, so Native Alaskans learned to hang strips of salmon in smoke. Fish dried and smoked this way remain good to eat for many months. You can enjoy this Alaskan treat in a modern way, and you don't even have to catch a fish or build a fire. Just buy a small package of smoked salmon (most grocery stores carry it).

You'll also want:

Crackers or thin slices of bread (pumpernickel bread is tasty)

Cream cheese or slices of your favorite cheese

Sliced dill pickles, lemon juice, seafood cocktail sauce

Spread cream cheese on a cracker or piece of bread. Now flake off a chunk of the smoked salmon, using a fork, and put it on top of the cheese. You can eat this delicious treat just as it is, but some people like to top it off with a slice of pickle, a squirt of lemon juice, or a dab of spicy seafood cocktail sauce. Use your imagination to come up with other combinations. Is this a snack or a meal? *That* depends on how much you eat!

Eskimos repair a fishing net near Kotzebue, north of the Arctic Circle.

completely to the old ways. But some people are trying to build a way of life that combines the best of the old and the new. Paul Ongtooguk, an Inupiat Eskimo, teaches Native studies in Kotzebue, the largest Eskimo community in the world. He hopes that the meeting of Native and white cultures can benefit both. "Here, in Alaska," he says, "we're trying to be optimistic that the three-hundred-year legacy of conflict between Western society and Native America will somehow turn out different. Alaskan Natives have the opportunity to become another downtrodden minority, or we have an opportunity to create a very successful synthesis [union] between our own society and Western society."

With growing pride in their heritage, Alaska's Natives have revived festivals and customs that were almost lost. In 1988, two thousand Inupiat Eskimos of the north coast gathered in Barrow for a *kivgiq*, or "messenger feast," a celebration that had not been held for seventy years. A *kivgiq* was an occasion for villages and individuals to exchange gifts. At the 1988 festival, gifts included a polar-bear skin given by a coastal community to a village in the Brooks Range and a pair of walrus tusks given by a hunter to a skilled carver. Feasts of traditional foods such as whale meat were alternated with storytelling and drumming. Dancers competed to imitate the movements of birds and animals.

The *kivgiq* was such a success that it is now held every year. A community leader explained, "There is a social and spiritual need inside us as Inupiat which can only be satisfied by our own traditions." An ancient tradition has been restored—except that instead of sending a messenger from village to village to spread word of the feast, today's Eskimos use fax machines.

GETTING AROUND

Getting around in Alaska can be a challenge. Although the Kenai Peninsula, the port of Valdez, and Fairbanks are linked by a network of highways, there are few other major roads in the state. A single gravel road leads from Fairbanks to Prudhoe Bay. The Alaska Highway is the only paved road into or out of the whole state.

Huge portions of Alaska cannot be reached by road. Alaskans call these roadless areas "the bush." They make an exception, though, for their capital city. Juneau is not considered part of the bush even though it can only be reached by sea or air—or on foot.

Anchorage and Fairbanks, and their suburbs, have streets like those in the Lower Forty-eight. In most communities, however, none of the streets go very far. A tour operator in Barrow remarked to a magazine reporter, "There are twenty-eight miles of road out here, and all of them dead-end."

TEN LARGEST CITIES

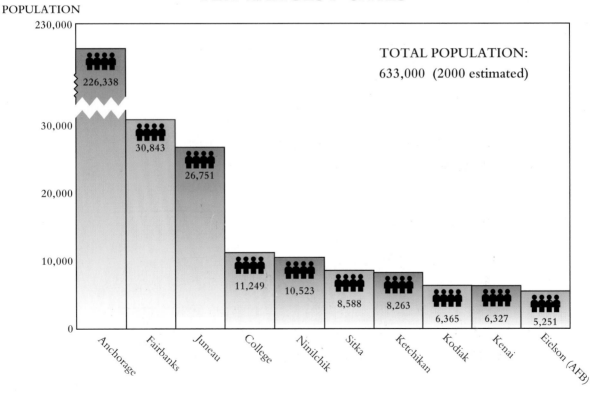

POPULATION

TOTAL POPULATION:
633,000 (2000 estimated)

230,000

226,338

30,000 — 30,843

26,751

20,000

11,249
10,523

10,000 — 8,588
8,263
6,365 6,327
5,251

0

Anchorage Fairbanks Juneau College Ninilchik Sitka Ketchikan Kodiak Kenai Eielson (AFB)

GIFTS FROM THE ESKIMOS

Do you have a parka? (Alaskans call it a PAR-kee.) A parka is a long, warm jacket that you pull on over your head. When white explorers came to Alaska, they saw the Eskimos wearing sturdy parkas made of caribou skin. The Aleut also made such coats—out of rainproof seal intestine, perfect for their wet climate. People around the world have adopted this useful design and wear parkas made of all kinds of materials, from wool to high-tech polyester fleece and breathable nylon.

The Eskimos also gave the world the kayak. This is a small, flat boat with a hide cover that seals the top of the boat around your waist to keep water out. You sit on the floor and steer with a double-bladed paddle. Boatbuilders have copied the Eskimo design in wood and fiberglass. Now kayakers in many countries enjoy paddling these fast-moving, nimble vessels.

Juneau is the only capital in the United States that cannot be reached by road. The only way to get there is by boat or airplane.

Alaskans have found ways to get around in the bush. All-terrain vehicles (ATVs) are popular in summer. When snow covers the ground, some people follow the traditional Eskimo practice of using dog teams to pull sleds, but snowmobiles are far more common today than sled dogs.

The backbone of bush transportation is the small plane. More people own and fly their own planes in Alaska than in any other state: One in every fifty-eight Alaskans is a registered pilot. Many of their planes are floatplanes, equipped to land on lakes.

Bush pilots are the heroes of rural Alaska. They deliver supplies, mail, and passengers to remote communities and settlers. For a price, they'll carry vacationers into the roadless wilderness—and out again a day, a week, or a month later. Bush pilot Stu Ramstad is a third-generation Alaskan. "I was born into it," he says. "There were people who created something where nothing existed before. That's the pioneering spirit, and that's the feeling I have."

Many Alaskans and visitors travel on the Alaska Marine Highway, a system of ferries that carry passengers and cars from port to port in southeastern, south-central, and southwestern Alaska. The Alaska Railroad carries passengers and freight between Seward and Anchorage in the south and Fairbanks in the interior.

EDUCATION AND RECREATION

Some families live so far from the nearest settlement that children cannot go to school. To make it easier for these youngsters to get an education, in 1939 the state began a program unlike any other in the country. It let children who wanted to study at home receive their lessons and turn in their homework by mail. The program continues today, using satellite television and the Internet in addition to the mail.

Most kids in Alaska, however, do attend school. About 124,000 Alaskan children attend public schools ranging from a large high school in Anchorage to one-room schoolhouses in small villages. Each year, about 33,000 students enroll in the University of Alaska, which has campuses in Anchorage, Fairbanks, Juneau, Sitka, and Ketchikan. The university system also includes more than a dozen

A computer tutors students in math.

smaller colleges across the state, from Nome to Unalaska.

The arts in Alaska include everything from opera in Anchorage to traditional Eskimo dancing in Kotzebue. The larger cities have many orchestras and theaters for Western-style performing arts. Native arts, too, are a lively part of Alaska's cultural life: Singers and dancers perform in the cities and at village gatherings, and artists produce fine arts and crafts, especially carvings and sculptures in wood, stone, bone, and jade, the state gem.

Alaska has no big-league sports teams, but it does have its own league of amateur baseball players, the Alaska Baseball League. Ice

The Inupiat and other Native groups are determined to keep their rich heritage of music and dance alive for future generations.

hockey is also popular—after all, there's plenty of ice. Local teams play in leagues, and professional teams sometimes visit.

In general, Alaskans are athletic, outdoorsy people. Many of them fish, ski, hike, canoe, snowshoe, or ice skate. Nordic cross-country skiing is especially popular because it does not require ski lifts or resorts. Cross-country skiers can practice their sport just about anywhere there's snow on the ground. The most "Alaskan" winter sport, however, is sled dog racing, also called mushing.

The Eskimos developed mushing as a way of traveling across snow, and early settlers learned it from them. Most people now rely on snowmobiles for serious winter transportation, but some Alaskans still run teams of husky or malamute sled dogs, for work or pleasure. Each year dozens of mushing races are held all over Alaska. The most famous of these events is the Iditarod Trail Sled Dog Race, which is held every March. The Iditarod commemorates a historic sled dog run of 1925, when mushers raced north from Nenana to Nome with medicine to save the town from an epidemic of disease. Balto, the lead dog on the team that carried the first load of medicine into Nome, became a hero.

Dogs and their mushers have to be heroic even to enter the Iditarod. They travel a 1,049-mile route from Anchorage to Nome, over mountains, burned-out stump forests, and Bering Sea ice, often during winter storms. The shortest time for any winner is 9 days, 2 hours, 42 minutes, and 19 seconds.

The Iditarod is famous, but it has stirred up controversy in recent years. The United States Humane Society and other animal-rights groups believe that it is too hard on the dogs. Because of their complaints, some big corporations stopped funding the race. The organizers have found new sponsors in Alaska and promise to keep the Iditarod going.

Yet even some Alaskans feel that the Iditarod is just a big tourist attraction, no longer genuinely Alaskan. Mike Doogan, a lifelong

Alaskan who writes for the *Anchorage Daily News*, says, "To me the Iditarod is another piece of faux [phony] Alaskana, a sort of gigantic painted gold pan with paws." In the race's early years, a third of the participants were Natives. Now the race is more professional, with more outsiders competing. In 1995, only one Iditarod musher was a Native, although mushing was originally a Native skill. Beverly Masek, an Athabascan Indian and a former Iditarod competitor who is a representative to the state legislature, claims that "race organizers haven't made much effort to involve Native communities."

The Iditarod race has become a symbol for the question that some Alaskans are asking about their state: How popular can it become, how much can we develop it, without losing the things that make it special?

Mushers and teams set off on the "last great race," the Iditarod Trail Sled Dog Race.

5 ADMIRABLE ALASKANS

The blanket toss at Point Hope began as a way for a hunter to spot distant game.

Alaska is a young state with a small population. It has not yet produced a president or a Nobel Prize winner—but someday it will. In the meantime, Alaska *has* produced colorful characters who became well known inside and outside their state. Some of them were born in Alaska. Others came from elsewhere to live and work in the Last Frontier.

THE ARTS

Alaska's wild beauty and exciting history have inspired many writers and artists. One of them was Rex Beach (1879–1949), whose tales of northern adventure were read all over the world. Beach lived in Stevens Village, which he used as the background for his novel *The Barrier*. In *The Iron Trail* he described the building of a railroad along the Copper River, and in *The Spoilers* he wrote about the gold rush at Nome.

Beach also wrote about Alaska's young and fast-growing salmon-fishing industry. *The Silver Horde*, published in 1909, tells of the hard, dangerous life of men who fought nature—and each other—to win a fortune from the sea. Here Beach describes what happened when millions of silver salmon started their journey up the Kalvik River:

Writer Rex Beach captured the crudeness and the heroism of life on the Alaskan frontier.

The main body of salmon struck into the Kalvik River on the first day of July. For a week past the run had been slowly growing, while the canneries tested themselves; but on the opening day of the new month the horde issued forth boldly from the depths of the sea, and the battle began in earnest. They came during the hush of the dawn, a mad, crowding throng from No Man's Land, to wake the tide-rips and people the shimmering reaches of the bay, lashing them to sudden life and fury. Outside, the languorous ocean heaved as smiling and serene as ever, but within the harbor a wondrous change occurred.

Sidney Laurence (1865–1940) used paint, not words, to

capture Alaska's glory. Born in New York City, Laurence studied painting there and in Paris. In 1903 he gave up art and went north to seek gold in Alaska. He failed to strike it rich, though, and worked for ten years as a cook, carpenter, and photographer.

In 1912 Laurence started painting again. He went on an expedition to Mount Denali, which had not yet been climbed, and returned with forty sketches of the continent's highest peak. Paintings based on the sketches aroused great interest in a 1915 exhibition in San Francisco; one of them now hangs in the

Sidney Laurence painted Mount McKinley, *the picture that made him famous, after accompanying an expedition to the mountain.*

National Museum of American Art of the Smithsonian Institution in Washington, D.C. Laurence continued to paint and sell Alaskan landscapes until his death in Seattle.

PUBLIC LIFE

An Eskimo born in 1911 in Point Hope, on the northwest coast of Alaska, grew into a great leader of the state's Native community. The baby's parents gave him both an Eskimo name, Sikvoan Weyahok, and an English name, Howard Rock. He was reared by an aunt and uncle, who taught him to fish, hunt, and carve walrus ivory. Rock began painting as a teenager. A teacher arranged for him to go to Oregon, where he studied art. Later he attended the University of Washington, planning a career as an artist.

In his third year of college, however, Rock dropped out of school to work for a company that made jewelry based on his designs. Over the years he made a lot of money, but by the age of forty he was miserable. He had become an alcoholic and lost all his money. He had lost touch with his roots and felt out of place in the non-Native world. Things became so bad that Rock planned to end his life.

During a farewell visit to Point Hope, however, he learned that the federal government was thinking about testing atomic bombs in the far north. Rock was furious, knowing that no one had listened to the Eskimos' views on the matter. He organized a Native protest against the plan, which the government dropped. At the same time, Rock returned to painting and jewelry making, this time working for himself and building a reputation as a fine artist.

Sikvoan Weyahok, known in English as Howard Rock, was an artist and a powerful voice for Native Alaskans in their struggle to retain their land and their dignity.

The Eskimos' protest against the atomic plan made Rock believe that Alaska's Native Americans could accomplish much if they communicated with each other and worked together. He decided to help. In 1962 he founded a newspaper called *Tundra Times*. Based in Fairbanks, the paper was a voice for the Aleuts, Eskimos, and Indians.

As a champion of Native rights, Rock helped file the first lawsuits for Native land claims. When the claims settlement act became law in 1971, he announced to all Natives, "Let us recognize the task that will fall on our shoulders. It will test the strength of our leaders as well as the rest of our people. We have proven that we can handle highly complex problems, such as the Alaska Native land claims. We must not do less in the future. We must meet it with confidence and then do more for the good of our people and those of tomorrow." Rock died five years later and was buried in a traditional Eskimo grave on the tundra near his birthplace.

Walter J. "Wally" Hickel, one of Alaska's best-known political figures, was born in Kansas in 1919 and went to Alaska at age twenty. "I didn't know a soul when I got off the boat in Seward," he later recalled. "I washed dishes in an Anchorage restaurant and at night slept on the floor of a cabin. When I was in that cabin, I thought twenty-five years ahead, and I knew where I was going." Hickel invested his money and grew rich by building hotels and other properties. A lifelong Republican, he was elected governor in 1966.

Hickel felt that Alaska needed more economic development and road building, especially in the Arctic. "It has always been said that Alaska is a vast storehouse of just about everything," he declared. "Now we must let the world know what we have and put it to use." Hickel was an enemy of the environmental protection movement of the 1960s. Environmentalists were upset in 1969 when President Richard Nixon made Hickel the secretary of the interior, putting him in charge of all public lands. The *New York Times* wrote, "Governor Hickel has indicated that he has little if any comprehension of the basic meaning and purposes of conservation. As chief steward of the nation's resources his inclination seems to be to put private profit ahead of the public interest."

In 1970 Hickel retired from government to work on his businesses. Twenty years later he returned to politics, elected to a second term as governor in 1990. His ideas about development were as strong as ever. In 1994 he filed a $29 billion lawsuit against the U.S. government because the government does not allow Alaska to build, mine, or harvest timber on protected federal land. The lawsuit was Hickel's way of asking for greater local control over federal land in Alaska.

Many Alaskans agree with Hickel about the need for more development, such as road building and mining in national parks. Those who don't agree sometimes use the term "Wally World" to

Walter Hickel served as secretary of the interior under President Nixon and as governor of Alaska for two terms. Hickel, who stood squarely for development and against conservation, cut a controversial and powerful figure in Alaskan politics.

describe some of Hickel's wilder ideas. For example, he has talked about digging a tunnel to Russia under the Bering Sea or operating an Arctic highway to Europe across the polar ice cap. "One thing about Wally," said an Anchorage man, "you can love him or you can hate him, but you can't ignore him. And he's never boring."

AN IDITAROD HERO

Susan Butcher is one of today's best-known and most admired Alaskans. She is the first woman to win the Iditarod Trail Sled Dog Race four times. Butcher was born in 1954 in Massachusetts and got her first dog when she was four. "I loved animals and the outdoors," she says of her childhood. "I felt very confined by city life. In the first grade I wrote things like 'I hate the city.' By the fourth grade it was stuff like 'I hate the city because society is ruining the earth for animals and people who live in the country are happier.'"

Butcher moved to Alaska in 1975. She began raising sled dogs and mushing. Three years later, she first competed in the Iditarod, and a year after that, she was one of the leaders of the first sled-dog team to reach the top of Mount Denali. Butcher was not the first woman to win the Iditarod. Libby Riddles took that honor in 1985, after Butcher had to drop out of the race because a moose attacked her and her dogs. But Butcher won in 1986, 1987, and 1988, the first person ever to win the race three years in a row. She won again in 1990. Today she raises dogs with her husband near Eureka, north of Fairbanks.

Susan Butcher is a hero to many women and men around the world who admire her strength, determination, love of the out-

Champion sled dog racer Susan Butcher has become a symbol of Alaskan spirit and strength.

doors, and skill with dogs. She sums up the ambitious Alaskan spirit when she says, "My goal was never to be the first woman or the best woman. My goal was to be the best sled-dog racer."

6 BY LAND, SEA, AND AIR

Glacier Bay

There's much to see in Alaska—but to see it all you'll have to travel by land, sea, and air, and you'll have to cover a *lot* of territory. "I was born in Alaska and I've been back eight times with my family," says seventeen-year-old Jason Valentine. "But still we've only seen a tiny part of what's up there."

Start your tour of Alaska the way many visitors do, with a trip north along the Inside Passage aboard a ferry or a cruise ship.

UP THE INSIDE PASSAGE

The Inside Passage is a trip through Alaska's history. As you travel the passage, you'll see Native arts, Russian buildings, gold-rush relics, and a modern state capital. Ketchikan, at the south end of the Passage, has the world's largest collection of totem poles, the work of Tlingit and Haida artisans. Petersburg, a fishing town settled by people from Norway, still has many buildings decorated with traditional Norwegian carved and painted designs called rosemaling. Each May residents of Petersburg hold a Little Norway festival.

Sitka was the center of Aleksandr Baranov's Russian-American empire. Today it is one of many places in southern Alaska where you can see Russian churches with their onion-shaped domes. The largest of these churches, St. Michael's Cathedral, has a famous

Totem poles in a Ketchikan park. An 1899 visitor to southeastern Alaska called the poles "the most striking feature" of every Tlingit and Haida village.

collection of Russian religious paintings known as icons. In this city you can see the New Archangel Dancers perform traditional Russian dances, and afterward you can wander through the old Russian cemetery.

In the mid-1970s Alaskans voted to move their state capital from Juneau to Willow, an easier-to-reach community not far from Anchorage. They have not yet gotten around to doing so, however, and Juneau remains the center of state government. It is also the

A guide in old-fashioned Russian clothing stands in front of the cathedral in Sitka.

site of the Alaska State Museum, which has a large collection of Native items, and the Juneau-Douglas City Museum, which tells the history of gold mining in the region. "It helps to be a mountain goat in Juneau," says travel writer Suzanne Hopkins. The city's streets aren't quite as hard to climb as the slopes where mountain goats roam, but Alaska's capital is built on the slopes of several steep hills.

Juneau is close to some of the most magnificent natural

wonders of the Inside Passage. Helicopters carry tourists to the nearby Mendenhall Glacier, where visitors walk around on the ice sheet. In Glacier Bay National Park, people watch from cruise ships—or from kayaks, if they're feeling adventurous—as huge chunks of ice break free from tidewater glaciers. Whales often surface near the boats.

Haines and Skagway, at the north end of the passage, have road connections to the Alaska Highway. Haines is famous for the 3,500 or so bald eagles that gather every winter to feed on salmon in the Chilkat River. It is the largest gathering of eagles in the world. Skagway was the gateway to the Yukon during the gold rush. The Klondike Gold Rush National Historical Park preserves the history of those wild and woolly days. Following the route taken by many prospectors on their way to the Yukon, visitors ride an old-fashioned train on an exciting and scenic trip over the White Pass.

SOUTH CENTRAL AND ANCHORAGE

Northwest of the Inside Passage is Wrangell-Saint Elias National Park. Six times bigger than Yellowstone, this park contains the largest wilderness area in the United States: 8.7 million acres, nearly twice the size of New Jersey. The park also contains nine of the highest peaks in the country and dozens of glaciers.

"Many of these valleys were filled with ice, and not very long ago," explains glacier expert Ed LaChappelle. "The cool northern climate here delayed its disappearance, and glaciers are receding as the great ice sheets did before them. So if you want a glimpse of

A midsummer pond forms on glaciers in Wrangell-Saint Elias National Park. Trickles from such ponds feed the park's fast-flowing mountain streams and rivers.

Many bald eagles, the American national bird, make their home in Alaska. Hundreds—sometimes thousands—of them gather to feed on salmon runs.

Left: A close-up look at the vast Mendenhall Glacier near Juneau

what New York and Wisconsin were like twelve thousand years ago, you can see it here." On his first visit to the park, travel writer Noel Grove said, "I can't get over the feeling that I'm the last person on earth. Or maybe the first."

Farther west is Anchorage, the city that boasts that it is "only half an hour from Alaska." Icebergs, glaciers, Native villages, gold mines, and wildlife refuges are all close at hand. From downtown you can see Mount Denali on the horizon. The mountain is so big that it looks close, but it is one hundred fifty miles away.

Anchorage has changed much since it began in 1914 as a cluster of tents for workers on the Alaska Railroad. Bob Atwood, publisher of the *Anchorage Times*, recalls early days in the city: "A dirt road ran around Anchorage. If you wanted to take a Sunday drive, you literally had to go around in circles." Now Anchorage, like other large cities, has problems of suburban sprawl and smog. But it also has many of Alaska's cultural attractions, such as the Southcentral Alaska Museum of Natural History, the Alaska Zoo, the Alaska Public Lands Information Center, and the Anchorage Museum of History and Art. Earthquake Park commemorates the quake of March 27, 1964, when parts of downtown sank thirty feet. The Oomingmak Musk Ox Co-op sells garments knitted by western Alaska Natives from *qiviut*, the underwool of musk oxen.

If you're in Anchorage in February, you'll get a chance to take part in one of Alaska's biggest festivals, the Anchorage Fur Rendezvous. The rendezvous began in 1936 to give fur trappers a place to sell their furs. Now it's a ten-day, citywide party that includes snowshoe races on downtown streets.

Even the tallest buildings of Anchorage are dwarfed by the Chugach Mountains in the background.

South of Anchorage, on Kamish Bay near the tip of the Kenai Peninsula, is the little town of Homer. Many artists have settled in cabins or houseboats in this picturesque community, with views of the ocean and the mountains. Homer has a number of art galleries and jewelry and craft shops, as well as the Pratt Museum, which contains exhibits about the area's history and wildlife. The bay is also famed as a fishing spot. Sport fishers come from around the world to catch its giant halibut.

THE SOUTHWEST

To many visitors, southwest Alaska means Kodiak Island. People visit Kodiak to see the famous Kodiak brown bears—most often viewed from the air during "flightseeing" trips. The town of Old Harbor, the site of the first Russian settlement in America, has a Russian Orthodox church more than two hundred years old. The Alutiiq Archaeological Repository and Museum in Kodiak, which opened in 1995, is dedicated to preserving the heritage of the

A woman cleaning a halibut in Homer, one of the sport-fishing capitals of the world

One tourist described Kodiak Island as "big, bleak, and beautiful." The island is known for its huge bears and its Aleut and Russian heritage.

Alutiiq people, who have lived on the island for 7,500 years.

In Katmai National Park on the Alaska Peninsula you'll find the Valley of Ten Thousand Smokes. After a volcano erupted there in 1912, vents in the valley floor spewed out steam hot enough to melt metal. Today only a few vents remain active. Katmai also has forests, rivers, lakes, glaciers, and plenty of Kodiak bears. The park can be reached only by air. There are almost no roads in southwestern Alaska. Ferries carry passengers to Kodiak Island and to several ports on the Alaska Peninsula. But ferry service ends at

Akutan, at the beginning of the Aleutian chain. People who want to go to the thinly populated islands must travel by private boat or plane.

NORTH TO THE FUTURE

Nome, the biggest city in northwestern Alaska, is reachable only by air. Once you get there, however, you can ride in a rented car along 250 miles of roads in the area, looking for bears, musk oxen, and other wildlife. You can also pan for gold on the beaches where the great gold rush started or take a short flight to eastern Russia. Because more than half of Nome's population is Eskimo, the city's shops are a good place to buy the clothing, jewelry, and carvings they make. The Carrie McLain Museum has exhibits about Eskimo culture and Nome's gold rush.

Kobuk Valley National Park contains something you might be surprised to see north of the Arctic Circle: twenty-five square miles of sand dunes. The sand was created by grinding glaciers thousands of years ago. Wind and river carried it to the Kobuk Valley. Gates of the Arctic National Park and Preserve, also north of the Arctic Circle, is sometimes called the "ultimate wilderness." It includes part of the Brooks Range as well as the Endicott and Schwatka Mountains, and marks the place where forest gives way to tundra. Caribou outnumber humans in this majestic landscape. The Arctic National Wildlife Refuge, farther north and east, gets even fewer visitors—about a thousand hikers and boaters a year. "But after all," says one Alaskan park ranger, "the refuge was created for the animals, not for us."

PLACES TO SEE

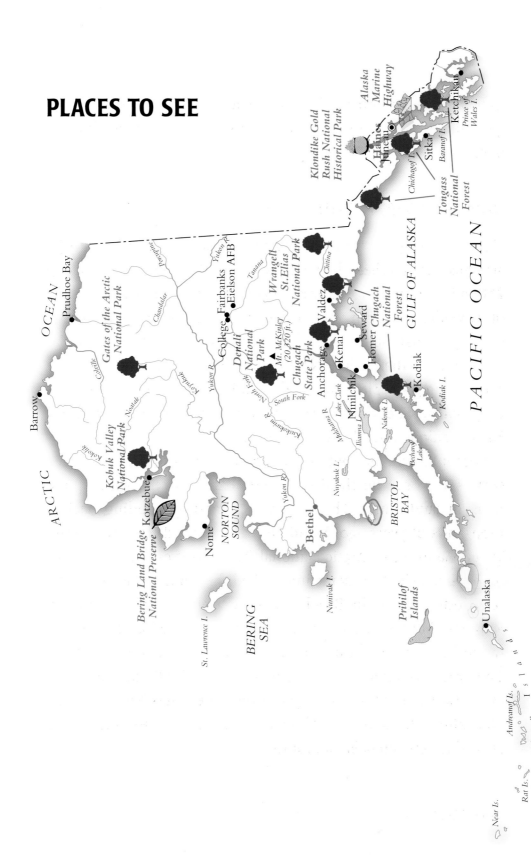

Klondike Gold
Rush National
Historical Park

Alaska
Marine Highway

Ketchikan

Prince of
Wales I.

Haines
Juneau

Chichagof I.

Sitka

Baranof I.

Tongass
National
Forest

GULF OF ALASKA

PACIFIC OCEAN

OCEAN

Prudhoe Bay

Noatak

Ikpikpuk

Chandalar

Colville

Kobuk

Gates of the Arctic
National Park

Yukon R.

Fairbanks
College
Eielson AFB

Tanana

Wrangell
St. Elias
National Park

Chitina

Valdez

Seward

Chugach
National
Forest

Barrow

Kobuk

Koyukuk

Yukon R.

Denali
National
Park

North Fork

Mt. McKinley
(20,320 ft.)

Chugach
State Park

South Fork

Anchorage

Kenai

Homer

Kodiak

Kobuk Valley
National Park

Kotzebue

Kuskokwim R.

Mulchatna R.

Lake Clark

Nimilchik

Kodiak I.

Bering Land Bridge
National Preserve

NORTON
SOUND

Nome

Yukon R.

Bethel

Iliamna L.

Ninyakuk L.

Naknek L.

Becharof
Lake

BRISTOL
BAY

ARCTIC

St. Laurence I.

BERING
SEA

Nunivak I.

Pribilof
Islands

Unalaska

Near Is.

Rat Is.

Andreanof Is.

Aleutian Islands

Caribou roam the north. Debate rages over whether wolves should be killed to protect the caribou.

THE HEART OF ALASKA

Fairbanks, Alaska's second-largest city, is the population center of the interior. The Alaska Highway leads thousands of visitors a year to Fairbanks and the smaller communities around it. The city's attractions include a forty-four-acre theme park called Alaskaland, the University of Alaska Museum, and the Milepost, a monument in downtown Fairbanks that shows the distances to such far-off points as Paris and Mexico City.

From Fairbanks, travelers can drive to Dawson City in Canada's Yukon Territory, to the Arctic Circle and beyond on the road to Prudhoe Bay, or to Anchorage and Valdez in the south. Most visitors head south. On the way to Anchorage they stop at Alaska's number-one tourist attraction, Denali National Park, hoping for a cloud-free glimpse of the highest peak in North America. The mountain, named for U.S. President William McKinley, is now often called by its Athabascan name, Denali, which means "the high one."

The park is both tundra and taiga (TIE-guh), or evergreen forest. It also is home to caribou, grizzly bears, moose, wolves, and other animals. Alaskans and the National Park Service are debating changes in how the park is run. For now, the number of vehicles and people that can enter the park on any given day is limited. Park rangers believe that limits are needed to give visitors a chance to see wildlife and feel the solitude and natural beauty of the wilderness. "I don't mind waiting to get in," said an eleven-year-old girl from California in 1994. "I don't even mind that we didn't get a look at the big mountain. I'd come back here every year if my mom and dad would bring me."

Many people who have visited Alaska feel the same way. And most of those who live there love their state. They want it to grow and prosper, and they worry about protecting the land and its resources. "Alaskans don't see the value of order, don't see the value of looking to the future," one Anchorage woman said in the 1970s, fearing that Anchorage's fast-growing sprawl of trailer parks and shopping malls would spread to other parts of the state.

It is hard for some Alaskans to understand that people all over the country and the world, even people who have never visited Alaska, also care very much about the state and what happens there. "Maybe I'll never live in Alaska," says Zachary Harris of

Portland, Oregon, "but I need to know that it's there, that it's one place we won't mess up. It belongs to all of us."

People who see "the great land" never forget it. Geographer Henry Gannett, who surveyed Alaska in 1904 for the federal government, wrote, "Its grandeur is more valuable than the gold or the fish or the timber, for it will never be exhausted."

A backpacker finds solitude in Denali National Park. After hiking for ten days in Denali, Joelle Myers of Anchorage said, "I live in Alaska, and still this was the adventure of a lifetime."

THE FLAG: There are a total of eight stars on the flag's blue background. The seven gold stars represent Alaska's gold resources and form the shape of the Big Dipper. The eighth star, alone in the upper right-hand corner, symbolises Alaska's location in the far north. Alaska's flag was adopted in 1927.

THE SEAL: The symbols on the seal represent Alaska's agriculture, fishing and mining. The seal also includes symbols of an iceberg, the northern lights, and Alaska's Native peoples. Alaska's state seal was adopted in 1913.

STATE SURVEY

Statehood: January 3, 1959

Origin of Name: Alaska comes from the Russian version of the Aleutian word *alyeska*, for "peninsula," "the great land," or "land that is not an island."

Nickname: Land of the Midnight Sun

Capital: Juneau

Motto: North to the Future

Bird: Willow ptarmigan

Fish: King salmon

Flower: Forget-me-not

Tree: Sitka Spruce

Gem: Jade

Willow ptarmigan

Forget-me-not

ALASKA'S FLAG

The poem "Alaska's Flag," by Marie Drake, was published in the Alaska School bulletin in 1935. Five years later her verses were set to music by Eleanor Dusenberry. In 1955 "Alaska's Flag" was adopted as the official state song.

Words by Marie Drake   **Music by Eleanor Dusenbery**

GEOGRAPHY

Highest Point: 20,320 feet above sea level, at Mount McKinley

Lowest Point: sea level

Area: 587,878 square miles including 17,502 square miles of inland water, but excluding 27,355 square miles of coastal water

Greatest Distance, North to South: Approximately 1,390 miles

Greatest Distance, East to West: Approximately 2,210 miles

Borders: The country of Canada lies to the east, the Arctic Ocean lies to the north, the Pacific Ocean borders southern Alaska, and the Bering Sea lies to the west

Hottest Recorded Temperature: 100°F at Fort Yukon on June 27, 1915

Coldest Recorded Temperature: −80°F at Prospect Creek, near Stevens Village, on January 23, 1971

Average Annual Precipitation: 55 inches

Major Rivers: Alsek, Chitina, Colville, Copper, Kobuk, Kuskokwim, Noatak, Selawik, Yukon

Major Lakes: Becharof, Clark, Lliamna, Minchumina, Naknek, Skilak, Teshekpuk, Tustumena

Trees: birch, black spruce, Sitka spruce, western hemlock, white spruce

Wild Plants: anemone, dwarf rhododendron, forget-me-not, lupine, marsh marigold, paintbrush

Animals: beaver, black bear, black-tailed deer, caribou, coyote, Dall sheep, grizzly bear, Kodiak brown bear, marten, mink, moose, mountain goat, otter, red fox, reindeer, wolf

Birds: bald eagle, duck, golden eagle, goose, grouse, hawk, loon, owl, surfbird, whistling swan

Fish: brook trout, chinook, cod, crab, halibut, harbor seal, herring, lake trout, northern pike, pink salmon, polar bear, porpoise, rainbow trout, sea lion, sea otter, shrimp, walrus, whale

Endangered Animals: blue whale, curlew, sea lion

Sea lion

TIMELINE

Alaskan History

c. 12,000 B.C.–7,000 B.C. Ancestors of Athabascan Indians cross Bering land bridge to Alaska

c. 7,000 B.C.–4,000 B.C. Eskimos and Aleuts migrate to Alaska from Siberia and Arctic Canada

1728 Vitus Bering passes north through the Bering Strait, proving that Asia and North America are separate

1741 On another expedition to explore northeastern Siberia, Bering sails into the Gulf of Alaska and lands on Kayak Island in Alaska

1778 British Captain James Cook surveys Alaskan coast

1784 Russians make a settlement at Three Saints Bay on Kodiak Island

1791 Captain George Vancouver, British navigator, charts southeast corner of Alaska

1799 Russia grants a monopoly of the Alaska fur trade to the Russian-American Company

1823 Father Ivan Veniaminov, Russian missionary, begins work among the Aleuts

1867 Secretary of State William Seward purchases Alaska from Russia for the United States for $7.2 million

1878 First commercial salmon cannery is built at Klawock

1884 District of Alaska is created

1896 Gold discovered in Klondike Basin of Canadian Yukon; unsuccessful prospectors in the Yukon turn toward Alaska, where some gold is found around Nome in 1898 and Fairbanks in 1902

1906 Alaska is allowed an elected delegate, without a vote, to Congress

1912 Alaska is organized as a territory of the United States

1917 Mount McKinley National Park is established

1924 Lieutenant Carl Ben Eielson flies first airmail to Alaska

1942 During World War II, the Japanese invade the Aleutian Islands

1943 Construction is completed on Alaska Highway, connecting Dawson Creek in Canada's British Columbia to the city of Fairbanks, Alaska

1954 First pulp mill in Alaska is completed at Ketchikan, giving a start to Alaska's large paper-producing industry

1957 Oil is discovered on Kenai Peninsula, making Alaska one of the world's most important oil-producing regions

1959 Alaska becomes the forty-ninth state

1964 A powerful earthquake strikes south-central Alaska

1977 The Trans-Alaska Pipeline, which transports oil from Prudhoe Bay to Valdez, is completed

1989 Exxon *Valdez* supertanker spills 11 million gallons of crude oil into Prince William Sound

ECONOMY

Agricultural Products: barley, dairy products, grass seeds, livestock, potatoes

Manufactured Products: fish products, foodstuffs, gasoline, and petro-chemicals

Natural Resources: copper, forests, gold, lead, mercury, natural gas, oil, silver, tin, zinc

Business and Trade: commercial fishing, forestry, fur trading, mining, tourism

Processing crab

CALENDAR OF CELEBRATIONS

Winter Sunrise After a long "night of darkness" from November to January, residents of Barrow are thrilled to see daylight again. The Winter Sunrise celebrates the welcome rays of the sun in late January.

Seward Polar Bear Jump Off You probably like jumping into a pool or lake to cool off during the hot days of summer, but this three-day event in January is not for the fainthearted. The main event of the Jump Off is a plunge into the frigid Resurrection Bay by the fearless members of the Polar Bear Club.

Fur Rendezvous Held in Anchorage in February, this 10-day carnival recalls the fur trappers who gathered in the city to sell their catch and to

socialize. During this celebration, more than 140 events from sled-dog races to softball games take place.

Annual Alaska Folk Fest Musicians and music lovers alike come to Juneau in March to listen to concerts, attend workshops, and to join in the various jam sessions. There are plenty of opportunities to dance as well as to listen to the music.

Iditarod Trail Sled Dog Race Also called the "Last Great Race on Earth," this popular race runs from Anchorage to Nome. The Iditarod follows part of two former dog-team mail routes, one of which became newsworthy in 1925 when diphtheria serum was rushed to Nome and saved the city from an epidemic outbreak. The trail runs close to 1,100 miles and has been declared a National Historic Trail.

Bering Sea Ice Classic You don't need any experience playing golf to participate in this lighthearted event on the ice. This five-hole tournament in Nome helps wind up the last week of the Iditarod.

Kodiak Crab Festival The focus of this festival is the crab, one of Alaska's most well-known seafoods, and the city's commercial fishing industry. It is held in Kodiak every year on Memorial Day weekend.

Solstice Baseball Game Do you think it's possible for a baseball game to run into the early hours of the morning? It happens once a year in Fairbanks when the semiprofessional team, the Goldpanners, treats fans to a midnight game on the weekend closest to the summer solstice.

World Eskimo-Indian Olympics Held in Fairbanks in July, these games focus on Eskimo tradition and culture.

Alaska State Fair The annual fair in Palmer, held in late August through Labor Day, is a spectacular sight. It features the legendary giant vegetables and nationally acclaimed fair gardens that yield over 20,000 flowers. There's plenty of family entertainment and delicious food for all ages to enjoy.

Bathtub Race You can win a statue of Miss Piggy and Kermit taking a bath by participating in this annual event in Nome. This unique race takes place at noon on Labor Day. Five-member teams, one of whom must be in the bathtub, race bathtubs mounted on wheels down Front Street. The rules state that the bathtub must be full of water at the beginning of the race and hold at least 10 gallons of water once it reaches the finish line.

STATE STARS

Aleksandr Baranov (1746–1819) was a Russian fur trader. He moved to Alaska in 1790 to head up a fur-trading company that later became the Russian-American Company. The Russian-American Company governed the Russian colony in Alaska.

E. L. Bartlett (1904–1968) was born in Seattle, Washington. His family relocated when he was one, and he grew up in Fairbanks, Alaska, where he was an editor for the local newspaper from 1924 to 1933. In 1944, he was elected to represent Alaska in the U. S. Congress. Bartlett fought hard for Alaskan statehood.

Rex Beach (1879–1949) was a prominent writer associated with Alaska. Beach lived in Stevens Village and used this Alaskan town as the background for his book *The Barrier*. Another of Beach's books, *The Spoilers*, gives a description of what Nome was like in its earlier days.

Vitus Bering (1681–1741), a Danish navigator, explored the continents of Asia and North America for Peter the Great of Russia. On his first trip to northern Siberia he concluded that the two continents were separated by water. During his 1741 expedition, Bering sighted Saint Elias in Alaska. The trip ended sadly when heavy fog forced him to land on Bering Island, where he died of scurvy.

Vitus Bering

Susan Butcher (1954–   ) moved to Alaska from Cambridge, Massachusetts, in 1975 to raise sled dogs. In 1978, she competed in her first Iditarod Trail Sled Dog Race, finishing nineteenth. She kept racing and, in 1986, won the Iditarod in record time. In 1988, she became the first person to win three Iditarod races in a row.

Anthony Diamond (1881–1953) came to Alaska in 1904 as a prospector and miner. He started practicing law in Alaska in 1913 and was later a member of the Alaska Territorial Senate. Diamond served as mayor of Valdez, Alaska, for nine years.

William Egan (1914–1984) was born in Valdez, Alaska. He served as a member of the house of representatives for the Alaska Territory and also as a one-term member of the senate. In 1958, Egan was elected the first governor of the state of Alaska. He was reelected two times, in 1962 and 1970.

Carl Eielson (1897–1929) came to Alaska in 1922 at the age of 25. He became a bush pilot and, in 1928, was the first person to fly over the Arctic Ocean. Eielson died when his plane crashed during a rescue mission to help an icebound Russian ship.

Carl Eielson

Ernest Gruening (1887–1974) introduced Alaska to the world through his books, which include *The State of Alaska* (1954) and *The Battle for Alaska Statehood* (1967). As a politician he served Alaska in various positions from 1938 until 1969. In 1939, the U.S. Congress appointed Gruening as governor of the Alaska Territory.

Walter Hickel (1919–   ) is a businessperson and public official. In 1940, he moved to Alaska and founded the Hickel Construction Company. In 1966, he was elected the first Republican governor of Alaska. In 1990, he ran again for governor, this time as an Independent, and was elected.

Bernard R. Hubbard (1888–1962) was a Jesuit scientist and lecturer. Born in San Francisco, California, he made his first trip to Alaska in 1927 to explore its glaciers. He made 10 other trips to Alaska during which he studied the language and customs of the Eskimos. He wrote two books: *Mush, You Malamutes* (1932) and *Cradle of the Storms* (1935).

Sheldon Jackson (1834–1909), educator and missionary, opened churches and schools across the country from 1859 to 1883. He did the same in Alaska in 1884. In 1891, he introduced reindeer to Alaska from their original habitats in northern Europe and Asia. These powerful animals were especially useful in the Arctic, where they could be trained to pull sleds through snow. Jackson served as the U.S. superintendent of public instruction in Alaska from 1885 to 1908.

Sidney Laurence (1865–1940) was an artist born in Brooklyn, New York, but often visited Alaska. Many of his paintings were of Native Americans and the Alaskan landscape. One of Laurence's paintings of Mount McKinley is displayed at the Smithsonian Institution in Washington, D.C.

Jack London (1876–1916) rose from poverty to become the most widely read novelist of his day. Eager for adventure, in 1897 he went to the Yukon to participate in the gold rush. His Alaskan experiences show up in some of his writings, including the famous *Call of the Wild*. This novel is a fictional account of a St. Bernard mix named Buck who was

kidnapped from his California home to lead a pack of sled dogs during the Yukon gold rush.

Jack London

Elizabeth Wanamaker Peratrovich

Elizabeth Wanamaker Peratrovich (1911–1958), a Native Alaskan, fought for Native rights in Alaska. As the president of Alaska Native Sisterhood, she fought to win voting and civil rights for Native Alaskans. Her speech to the state legislature in 1945 regarding Native rights resulted in a law that banned discrimination against Natives.

Gregory Shelikov (1747–1795) was a Russian merchant and fur trader who founded Alaska's first trading post, on Kodiak Island.

Don Simpson (1945–1996) was a movie producer from Anchorage who worked on such hit films as *Top Gun* and *Flashdance*.

Don Simpson

Father Ivan Veniaminov (1797–1879) worked for 10 years among the Aleut peoples. During this time he learned their language and customs. Father Veniaminov translated parts of the Bible and several prayers and hymns into the Aleut language.

Sikvoan Weyahok (Howard Rock) (1911–1976) was born in Point Hope, Alaska. He was a painter and sculptor who in 1962 founded the *Tundra Times* newspaper. This paper became the voice of Alaska's Native groups.

TOUR THE STATE

Inside Passage (southeastern coastal cities) The Inside Passage is Alaska's state ferry liner system. Ferry liners carry cars and passengers from Rupert, British Columbia, and Seattle, Washington, to Alaska's southeastern coastal cities. In addition to the spectacular scenery, each town along the route offers special attractions.

Ketchikan (south) Known as the Salmon Capital of the World, Ketchikan also has the world's largest collection of totem poles.

Metlakatla (near Ketchikan) Visitors to this Tsimshian Indian village can also view a sawmill and a salmon cannery.

Sitka (south) A large number of Russian churches can be found in this city located on Alaska's southeastern coast. The largest of these churches is St. Michael's Cathedral, which contains a number of Russian religious paintings.

Sitka National Historic Park (near Sitka) This is a favorite visitors' destination in the historic city of Sitka. Families can enjoy the wildlife sanctuary, a cultural center for Native American and Russian history, and a Tlingit totem park.

Juneau (south) Alaska's state government and its cultural hub is in the city of Juneau. The Alaska Historical Library and Museum located here has the most complete Eskimo art collection in the United States.

Mendenhall Glacier (north of Juneau) You can land a helicopter here and walk on this magnificent glacier that measures 14 miles long and 4 miles wide. Gaze down into the breathtakingly deep crevasses and cracks and, when you get thirsty, scoop a drink of water from a swift glacier stream.

Skagway (at head of Lynn Canal) Step back into time to the exciting gold-rush days. The city's seven-block boardwalk features shops and saloons that date from the gold rush or were built in the style of that period. You can see gold-rush artifacts and native cultural displays at the granite Trail of '98 Museum.

Glacier Bay National Park (southeastern coast) Made a national park in 1925, this park includes many enormous glaciers. Visitors also have opportunities to watch whales and seals at play.

Anchorage (southern coast) Located in southern Alaska, Anchorage is one of the state's most important cities. Over 40 percent of all Alaskans live here. In spite of its size, Anchorage is only a short distance from some of the state's most beautiful natural scenery, such as glaciers, wildlife refuges, and Mount McKinley.

Homer (southern coast) Many artists call this small town near the tip of the Kenai Peninsula home. Visitors can browse the art galleries, jewelry stores, and craft shops. Fishers from around the world come to Homer to catch giant halibut.

Valdez (southern coast) This ice-free port is the southern terminus of the Trans-Alaska Pipeline. It also includes Columbia Glacier, Keystone Canyon, and Bridal Veil Falls.

Seward (on Resurrection Bay) This ice-free port is the gateway to the Kenai Peninsula and the interior of Alaska. The headquarters for big-game hunters, the city is named for Secretary of State William Seward, who purchased Alaska for the United States from Russia.

Katmai National Park (on the Alaska Peninsula) Katmai National Park is the home of the world's largest brown bears. In 1912, Mount Katmai erupted, leaving vents in the mountain's valley floor from which hot steam flows. This dramatic area, known as the Valley of Ten Thousand Smokes, is a favorite trek for hikers.

Kodiak (Kodiak Park) Visitors take a ferry to explore the state's oldest community and sixth largest city. You can find a wealth of Russian and Native artifacts in the Baranov Museum, Alaska's oldest structure. The Russian Orthodox Church, built in 1794, is Alaska's first church.

Nome (northern Alaska on the Bering Sea) This city is reachable only by air. Tourists can pan for gold in this historic gold-rush town, or they can buy Eskimo clothing, jewelry, or carvings.

Kotzebue (western coast) One of the world's largest Eskimo villages, Inupiat Eskimos make up 80 percent of its population. Many residents practice traditional subsistence lifestyles and use handmade fishing boats to make a living.

Barrow Point (northern Alaska) Barrow Point is the northernmost point in Alaska. Nearby is a memorial to American entertainer Will Rogers and his pilot, Wiley Post. Both died in a plane crash near Barrow Point.

The Arctic National Wildlife Refuge (northern Alaska) Although few visitors find their way to this wilderness area in the far northeast, this refuge is home to some of Alaska's abundant wildlife, including the caribou, oxen, and migratory shorebirds.

Northern Lights (northern Alaska) The aurora borealis, or northern lights, is a band of color that stretches across the sky, occurring most frequently above 60 degrees north latitude. Alaska's residents and visitors never stop being fascinated by this beautiful sight.

FUN FACTS

Alaska's flag was designed by a 13-year-old boy.

America purchased Alaska for $7.2 million, or about 2¢ per acre.

Alaska's general coastline, which measures 6,640 miles, is longer than the coastlines of all the other states combined.

Inland water in Alaska covers an area larger than the states of Vermont and New Hampshire combined.

On March 27, 1964, a massive earthquake, one of the most powerful ever recorded in North America, hit Alaska. In some parts of Anchorage, pavement fell 30 feet in just a few seconds.

Alaska has the 16 highest mountain peaks in the United States, including Mount McKinley, which is the highest mountain peak in all of North America.

FIND OUT MORE

GENERAL STATE BOOKS

Editors of Milepost. *Alaska A to Z.* Bellevue, Wash.: Vernon Publications, 1993.

Fradin, Dennis. *From Sea to Shining Sea: Alaska.* Chicago: Childrens Press, 1994.

Heinrichs, Ann. *America the Beautiful: Alaska.* Chicago: Childrens Press, 1991.

Johnston, Joyce. *Alaska.* Minneapolis: Lerner Publications, 1994.

Smith, Carolyn, editor. *The Alaska Almanac: Facts about Alaska.* 18th edition. Seattle, Wash.: Alaska Northwest Books, 1994.

Thompson, Kathleen. *Alaska.* Milwaukee: Raintree Publishers, 1988.

BOOKS ABOUT ALASKAN PEOPLE, PLACES, OR HISTORY

Alexander, Bryan, and Cherry Alexander. *An Eskimo Family.* Minneapolis: Lerner Publications, 1985.

Bonvillain, Nancy. *The Haidas.* Brookfield, Conn.: Millbrook Press, 1994.

Carr, Terry. *Spill: The Story of the Exxon Valdez.* New York: Franklin Watts, 1991.

Dolan, Ellen M. *Susan Butcher and the Iditarod Trail.* New York: Walker, 1993.

Gruening, Ernest, editor. *An Alaskan Reader, 1867–1967.* New York: Meredith Press, 1966.

Jenness, Aylette, and Alice Rivers. *In Two Worlds: A Yup'ik Eskimo Family.* Boston: Houghton Mifflin, 1989.

McPhee, John. *Coming into the Country.* London: Hamish Hamilton, 1978.

Morgan, Lael. *Alaska's Native People.* Edmonds, Wash.: Alaska Northwest Publishing, 1979.

———. *Art and Eskimo Power: The Life and Times of Alaskan Howard Rock.* Fairbanks, AK: Epicenter Press, 1988.

Newman, Shirlee P. *The Inuit.* New York: Franklin Watts, 1993.

People of the Ice and Snow. Alexandria, Va.: Time-Life Books, 1994.

Ragan, John David. *Explorers of Alaska.* New York: Chelsea House, 1992.

Younkin, Paula. *Indians of the Arctic and Subarctic.* New York: Facts on File, 1992.

VIDEOS

Alaska: A History in Five Parts. Anchorage: University of Alaska, n.d.

Alaska Portrait. Alaska Video Publishing, n.d.

Alaska Rainforest: The Tongass. Juneau: KTOO-TV and Alaska Natural History Association, n.d.

Alaska's Denali Park. Alaska Video Postcards, n.d.

Bush Pilots of Alaska. Publishers Choice Video, 1996.

Kenai Fjords National Park. Alaska Video Postcards, n.d.

Predators of the Wild: Grizzly Bear. Survival Anglia Productions, 1992.

Traveling the Alaska Highway. Sky River Films, 1996.

Yukon Passage. National Geographic, 1996.

WEBSITES

You can find the state of Alaska Home Page at http:www.state.ak.us/gov on the World Wide Web. Another excellent Internet resource is http://www.ptialaska.net, which has dozens of links to informative Websites about Alaska.

INDEX

Page numbers for illustrations are in boldface.